Umbrella Guide to
Skiing in Alaska
Downhill and Cross-Country

by Elizabeth Tower

To Jack & Martha
Old friends and
fellow authors
Betsy Tower
10/28/97

Published by Epicenter Press, Inc.

UMBRELLA
BOOKS

Umbrella Books™ are a series of regional travel guides focusing on destinations in Alaska, Washington, Oregon, and California.

Editor: Christine Ummel
Cover design: Elizabeth Watson
Front cover photo: Downhill skiing at Eaglecrest Ski Area near Juneau. Photo by Mark Kelley.
Back cover photos:
 Top: Snowboarder at Alyeska Ski Resort. Courtesy of Alyeska Ski Resort, photo by John L. Kelley.
 Middle: Cross-country skiers near Anchorage. Courtesy of Anchorage Convention and Visitors Bureau, photo by Tom Bol.
 Bottom: Tram at Alyeska Ski Resort. Courtesy of Alyeska Ski Resort, photo by Ken Graham Photography.
Maps: Rusty Nelson
Inside design: Sue Mattson
Printer: Best Book Manufacturers

Text © 1997 Elizabeth Tower
ISBN 0-945397-45-3
Library of Congress Catalog Card Number: 97-061160

To order single copies of UMBRELLA GUIDE TO SKIING IN ALASKA, mail $12.95 (Washington residents add $1.11 state sales tax) plus $3 for shipping and handling to: Epicenter Press, Box 82368, Kenmore, WA 98028. BOOKSELLERS: Retail discounts are available from our trade distributor, Graphic Arts Center Publishing Company™, Portland, Ore., phone 800-452-3032.

PRINTED IN CANADA
First Printing August 1997
10 9 8 7 6 5 4 3 2 1

Contents

Acknowledgments

I would like to thank the following people for providing valuable information about the early history of Alaska ski areas and programs:

Duane Luedke, for sharing his clippings about the Anchorage Ski Club, the Arctic Valley ski area (Alpenglow), and Alyeska;

Dick Mize, for his written information on the early history of the Anchorage School District cross-country ski programs, the Army biathlon training program, and the Anchorage cross-country ski trails;

Jane McNeely Parrish, for sharing her research papers, "Respecting Our Routes," which told the history of the University of Alaska Fairbanks ski trails and the Skarland Ski Trails, and "A Management Plan for Birch Hill Recreation Area," which detailed the history of the Birch Hill cross-country trails;

Bob Janes, Juneau Ski Club historian, for the clippings and letters pertaining to the history of the Juneau Ski Club and the Juneau ski areas that preceded the current Eaglecrest development;

Pat Murphy, park ranger for the Independence Mine State Historical Park, Hatcher Pass Management Area, for relating the history of skiing in the Hatcher Pass area;

And Joyce Weaver Johnson and her husband, Barry, for the excellent work they do in publishing *Nordic Skier*, the newsletter of the Nordic Ski Association of Anchorage, Inc. This monthly publication contains current information on Anchorage area ski races, tours, cabins, and lodges, as well as articles about equipment, instruction and training programs, technique, and the achievements of local skiers. Articles on ski jumping, biathlon, and skijoring are also featured. A membership in the NSAA is often a worthwhile investment if only to receive the newsletters.

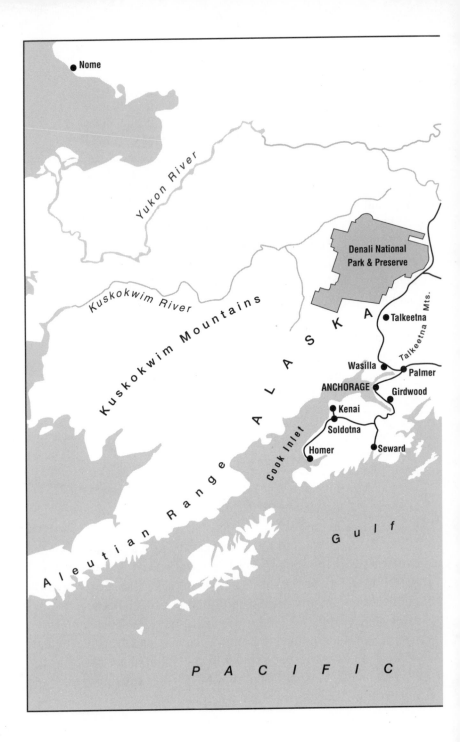

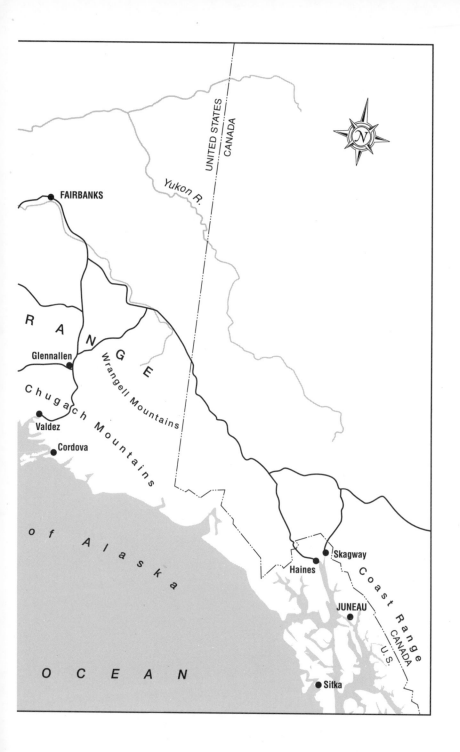

Introduction

For people who enjoy skiing, winter can be the best season of the year in Alaska. Groomed, lighted cross-country trails traverse major cities, and wilderness lodges set miles of touring trails. Cabins can be rented along winter trails in national forests and state parks. Although only a few of Alaska's snow-covered mountains are equipped with ski lifts, helicopters and snowcats are starting to offer access to myriads of virgin ski runs.

Skiing has greatly grown and changed since it was first brought to Alaska just over one hundred years ago. Native people in North America did not use skis or domesticate caribou for use as pack animals prior to contact with Europeans, relying instead on snowshoes and domesticated wolves to pull their sleds. In 1892, Presbyterian missionary Sheldon Jackson arranged for the introduction of reindeer to Alaska, and the reindeer were accompanied by Laplanders with skis.

Some of these Scandinavians were among the fortunate prospectors who discovered gold on the Seward Peninsula and set off the rush to Nome in 1899. Although prospectors elsewhere in Alaska and the Klondike occasionally fashioned skis to help them get around in the deep winter snow, the Scandinavian prospectors who flocked to Nome showed that skiing could also be recreational.

On February 12, 1904, *The Nome Semi-Weekly News* described the new sport: "Of all the winter sports there is none more exciting, none more exhilarating and none more healthful than the Norwegian sport of skiing. Up hill and down dale the skiers glide, — the long wooden strips slipping over the snow and the miles pass away with scarce an effort. The sport is fast taking hold of the people of Nome and during the past week at least twenty ladies and gentlemen have purchased skis and on every pleasant afternoon numbers of couples

Members of the Nome Ski Club, their skis stuck in the surrounding snow, enjoy a social gathering in 1904.

may be seen about the hills — some more or less proficient — and many humorous incidents arise."

Pictures of early skiers in Nome show them propelling themselves with only one pole, which must have been reasonably efficient since the winner of a ten-mile race covered the course in an hour and a half.

Jumping contests were held along with the cross-country races. In March 1905, *The Nome Semi-Weekly News* announced that the Sons of the North, a "social and fraternal organization composed of members of the Scandinavian races," had constructed a ski jump on the left limit of Dry Creek with a high platform so that "devotees of this exciting sport" could glide down with the "speed of chain lightning." Leonhard Seppala, who later won international fame as a sled dog racer, was one of the early ski jumping champions in Nome.

Skiing continued to increase in popularity in Nome for the next decade. A picture of soldiers at Fort Davis in 1912 shows that the Army supplied the troops with skis — and two poles. High school yearbooks of that era include pictures of both boys and girls racing on skis.

Although dog mushing eventually replaced skiing as the primary sport on the Seward Peninsula in the 1920s, Nome had served as the successful birthplace of skiing in Alaska. When gold strikes and railroad construction elsewhere in Alaska lured Scandinavian immigrants to new towns, they took their skis with them, erected small ski jumps, and organized nordic events, thus spreading the sport of skiing throughout the territory. Those early Scandinavian skiers were fortunate to have a single pair of skis to use for all occasions. If they failed to bring equipment with them from Scandinavia, they had to import skis or fashion them out of locally available wood and construct their own leather bindings.

Over the ensuing century, however, skiing has become specialized, and ski equipment has been modified to perform well under differing conditions. The average recreational skier in Alaska may use six to eight sets of skis and boots to take full advantage of the variety of skiing opportunities Alaska has to offer.

Ski lifts provide access to steep slopes, making firm boots, rigid safety bindings, and sharp-edged skis necessary for alpine skiing. Since snow conditions vary, downhill skiers often use short, wide skis for deep powder and narrower, sharp skis for carving on ice. A set of old "rock skis" may be kept to use early in the season when snow cover is sparse. Two or three pairs of skis will suffice for the recreational downhill skier, but the aspiring racer may buy different skis for downhill, giant slalom, and slalom races.

Most serious cross-country skiers now have at least two sets of skis, boots, and poles — one set for the new "skating" technique and another for the classical "striding" technique. Backcountry touring requires a sturdier set of skis with cable bindings. Skis with

"NOME, ALASKA — The ski race on Anvil Creek last Sunday was attended by a large number of people. The day was beautiful, and many people went for the ride as much as to see the ski race. But the race was none the less interesting. It was a contest between women, and a man dressed as a Lapp woman caused consternation in the ranks of the fair contestants by outdistancing all competitors. But he was barred from the prizes, which were won by Mrs. E. Kjelsberg and Mrs. T. Lehmann, who reside on the Sandspit. Mrs. Kjelsberg won the first prize, a medal, by running two miles in 17 minutes and 55 seconds. Mrs. Lehmann covered the distance in 19 minutes and 30 seconds and won a medal. The booby prize was won by Mrs. Field, whose time was 27 minutes and 35 seconds. There was a lot of fun in skiing down hill, and some long jumps. Mr. Sverdrup won the honors in the jumping contest, but Mr. Groven and some of the other champions were not present. The biggest jump last Sunday was 47 feet."

— *The Nome News*, Tuesday, April 23, 1903

no-wax, fish-scale bottoms are handy for use in heavy new snow. Any skiers wishing to attempt backcountry downhill skiing will find that modern telemark skis, boots, bindings, and climbing skins can increase their success and enjoyment. Ski jumping and ski mountaineering also require specialized equipment.

Snowboarding has become very popular in Alaska, accounting for almost half of the business in some downhill areas. Although snowboarders were not allowed on ski lifts for several years, they are welcome everywhere now. More and more snowboarders are venturing into the backcountry, using snowshoes to climb and specially designed packs to carry their boards. Although the majority of boarders are young boys, girls are also taking up the sport, and some adventurous adult skiers are adding snowboards to their garage equipment racks.

Alaska offers skiers considerable variety in terrain and climate. The northern region centering around Fairbanks is the coldest, with rolling terrain and early snow. The Southeast region around Juneau is mountainous and temperate, with heavy snow and frequent winter rain. Probably the most advantageous climate is found in Southcentral Alaska, including Anchorage, the Matanuska-Susitna valley, the Kenai Peninsula, and Prince William Sound. There the temperatures are moderate and consistent, usually with adequate snow cover by Thanksgiving, and the varied terrain is appropriate for both alpine and nordic skiing.

A skier in Alaska should always be aware of three potential dangers — frostbite, hypothermia, and avalanches. Frostbite can occur whenever the temperature is below zero degrees Fahrenheit or when the chill factor is extreme. Precautions must be taken to protect the nose and exposed ear lobes. Hypothermia is a threat to backcountry skiers who encounter weather and fatigue that they are not prepared for. Downhill ski areas in Alaska have good avalanche control programs, but the backcountry tourer or telemark skier must take personal responsibility for recognizing potentially dangerous snow conditions. Of course, skiing always involves some danger of injury, and all who participate do so at their own risk.

The history of various ski areas shows that Alaska has come a long way toward reaching its potential as a mecca for all types of skiers. Growth in downhill skiing was particularly strong in the 1960s and 1970s, when Anchorage served as a major refueling stop on many international airline routes between Europe and Asia. Air France, SAS, KLM, Lufthansa, British Airways, and Japan Air Lines all had regular flights into Anchorage. As a result, their flight crews and some international tourists discovered the wonderful skiing opportunities around Anchorage.

Today the downhill ski areas near Anchorage and Juneau are small compared to large developments in the western United States and Canada, but they have challenging terrain and are producing international champions. The cross-country trails in Anchorage and Fairbanks are probably the best designed and maintained in North America. The backcountry skiing, which is recognized as the best in the world, may prove to be one of Alaska's greatest future assets in winter recreation.

It's uncertain how quickly skiing will continue to grow as a sport in Alaska. With the end of the Cold War in the 1980s, international airlines can now fly over the former Soviet Union and therefore no longer need to stop in Anchorage. All the international airlines stopped running passenger flights into Anchorage. This has decreased the international market for Alaska's ski areas, forcing them to depend largely on local business.

As a result, numerous grandiose proposals to develop large ski areas in Alaska have been discarded because market analysis indicated that there was not enough demand to make them profitable. A few years ago, an Austrian entrepreneur envisioned an extensive alpine ski area just north of Anchorage in the Eagle River valley. A Japanese syndicate has discarded its initial ambitious dreams for a world-scale development in the Hatcher

Pass area north of Anchorage, but local developers still hope to obtain funding for a scaled-down resort.

In 1997 the north face of Mt. Alyeska was opened to skiers; the Alyeska Ski Resort may extend into adjoining terrain if increased skiing pressure justifies further enlargement. In the meantime, helicopter and sno-cat operators are providing intrepid skiers with more access to virgin slopes in the Talkeetna and Chugach mountain ranges. Anchorage came close to securing the Winter Olympics in both 1992 and 1994 and may try again in the future — but not for several years, since Salt Lake City will host the Olympics in 2002.

Today the people of Alaska, especially Anchorage, are promoting skiing as one of many wintertime activities for visitors to the area in the traditional off-season for tourism. Future growth of Alaska skiing may depend on their ability to persuade skiing tourists, from the Lower 48 and around the world, that winter is a glorious time to visit Alaska.

Underneath Flattop Mountain, a cross-country skier heads down a lighted loop trail in Far North Bicentennial Park.

1. ANCHORAGE

Anchorage's 250,000 residents don't need to leave town to enjoy hours of world-class cross-country skiing on trails that are regularly groomed for both classical diagonal striding and skating. This extensive trail system is maintained jointly by the Nordic Skiing Association and the Municipal Department of Parks and Recreation, with the municipality assuming responsibility for the Russian Jack Springs trails and the multiple-use Chester Creek and Coastal trails. The Nordic Skiing Association of Anchorage grooms and maintains over 115 kilometers of trails, including those in Kincaid Park, in Far North Bicentennial Park, at Bartlett High School, and at Alaska Pacific University and the University of Alaska Anchorage (the Mahaffey Trails).

Nordic Skiing Association of Anchorage (NSAA)

My family had the rare privilege of participating in the development of cross-country skiing in Anchorage from its beginnings in the early 1960s. We first saw cross-country skiers during a weekend ski trip to Independence Mine in the Talkeetna Mountains, sixty miles north of Anchorage. Fort Richardson, on the outskirts of Anchorage, had been chosen as the site for the U.S. Army Biathlon training center in 1958, and team members were enjoying early snow in the Hatcher Pass area.

The next Christmas I asked for cross-country ski equipment. This was not an easy wish to grant, but my husband managed to

17

find a set of Swedish skis at one city sports store and a pair of Norwegian boots at another. Later that year, a friend imported a set of equipment from Norway for my husband. An enterprising skier imported some Karhu skis from Finland, so we were able to outfit our oldest daughter. We skied on hillside pole lines and along the Alaska Railroad tracks from our downtown home to the old Forest Park golf course.

The following October, I heard that Clark Junior High was holding a Halloween dance to raise money to buy downhill ski equipment for the school. I suggested that cross-country equipment might be more practical. Joe Kalla, the physical education teacher, made the same suggestion and convinced the principal. The school purchased surplus Army cross-country skis, which shop teacher John Kerr cut down to make training skis for physical education classes and a cross-country racing team.

Kalla gave physical fitness tests to the seventh- and eighth-graders and persuaded some of the best runners to learn to cross-country ski. By the time the state high school championship took place in late February, his skiers were ready. An eighth-grader from Clark won the state championship. Two members of that first Clark Junior High team went on to outstanding careers in cross-country skiing. Tom Besh would serve as athletic director and ski coach for the University of Alaska Anchorage until his untimely death in an airplane accident. Ken Aligood, the eighth-grader who won the 1963 championship, became an Olympic biathlon competitor and U.S. Biathlon coach.

Other schools followed Clark's example by acquiring surplus Army skis and integrating cross-country skiing into the junior high physical education program. Experienced skiers, like former Olympian Dick Mize, coached high school and junior high teams, which competed against teams from Fairbanks, Juneau, and Homer. Within several years, Alaska was producing national champions.

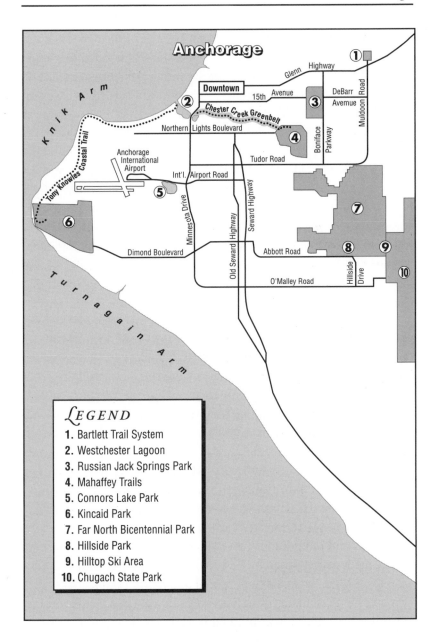

LEGEND

1. Bartlett Trail System
2. Westchester Lagoon
3. Russian Jack Springs Park
4. Mahaffey Trails
5. Connors Lake Park
6. Kincaid Park
7. Far North Bicentennial Park
8. Hillside Park
9. Hilltop Ski Area
10. Chugach State Park

On January 14, 1964, parents and friends of the school cross-country teams organized the Nordic Ski Club of Anchorage to assist in holding races and developing trails in the Anchorage area. The first president, Col. Eric Wikner, had formerly served as assistant commandant of the Mountain Training Center at Fort Carson in Colorado.

The Nordic Ski Club, which was incorporated in 1972 as the Nordic Skiing Association of Anchorage (NSAA), has continued to grow and now is so large that monthly meetings are no longer held. Instead the NSAA conducts its business through specialized committees, which focus on conservation, jumping, lands and trails, membership, racing, the Ski Train, telemarking, tours, huts, biathlon, the newsletter, track pins, Ski Patrol, the Trail-of-the-Week, and publicity. Many of those who participated in the early Nordic Ski Club races as children now help run the association's programs.

Besides working closely with the Anchorage Municipal Department of Parks and Recreation to provide trail grooming and instruction programs, the NSAA publishes a monthly Nordic Newsletter to keep its membership well informed about races, tours, trail development, land issues, and current equipment. Because its programs are entirely dependent on voluntary contributions, nordic skiers who use Anchorage trails are asked to purchase a $50 trail pin each year.

The NSAA office, at 316 Lynwood Drive, is open Tuesday, Wednesday, and Friday during the ski season. For more information, write to: P.O. Box 10-3504, Anchorage, AK 99510-3504. Phone 907-276-7609 or call the Ski Trail Hotline at 907-248-6667.

Tour of Anchorage

Every spring for the past ten years, the Tour of Anchorage loppet race has been run in early March. The race, which takes top competitors about two hours to complete, starts on the Hillside Trail System at Service High School on the east side of the city and leads

ELIZABETH TOWER

Skiers line up at Service High School for the start of the Tour of Anchorage, a 50-km race across the city.

across Anchorage to Kincaid Park on the west side. This 50-kilometer course passes through all of the city's major cross-country areas, in state and municipal parks and on college campuses. These are connected by dedicated multi-use trails; roads are crossed using underpasses and overpasses.

Hillside Trail System

The Tour of Anchorage starts on the Hillside Trail System in Far North Bicentennial Park, which also connects with the extensive trail system of Chugach State Park. The Hillside trails were established in 1971, when a small group of Nordic Ski Club members realized the need for sports programs at the Service-Hanshew school complex and planned five kilometers of trails on park land adjacent to the school. In 1972 the present 5-km Richter Loop and

21

2.5-km Ridge Loop were added, and the original trail was widened and modified. Further modification was necessary following a forest fire in 1974.

The municipality provided funds for widening and lighting 2.5 kilometers of the trail in 1978. In 1985 the Nordic Skiing Association designed and constructed the 7.5-km Spencer Loop and, in 1993, municipal park bonds made it possible to light another 2.5 kilometers of trail. Thanks to contributions from the Junior Nordic League in 1995, lighted trails now connect Service High School with the other lighted loops.

In this trail system, all lighted loops are intermediate in difficulty and are wide enough to accommodate both diagonal striding and skating. A section of the lighted trail that was burned over allows for beautiful views of Mt. Spurr and Mt. Redoubt, particularly at sunset. This burned-over section provides resident moose with tender young willows to munch on. Although skiers frequently encounter moose in this area, the moose are so accustomed to skiers that they are rarely a problem.

More of a challenge, the Spencer Loop is hilly and difficult, but has wonderful views of Anchorage and the mountains beyond, Mt. Susitna and Mt. McKinley. The Richter Loop and the Ridge Loop are narrow and only groomed for diagonal skiing, with some downhill sections that might intimidate a beginning skier.

Far North Bicentennial Park

Between the Hillside trails and campus trails to the north, the Tour of Anchorage trail leads through Far North Bicentennial Park. This 5,000-acre tract in the center of the Municipality of Anchorage was used by the military as an auxiliary airfield during World War II. When it was declared surplus after the war, the property passed to the Bureau of Land Management (BLM), which built administrative offices there and used the Campbell Air Strip for training firefighters. Old military tank trails on the property have been used

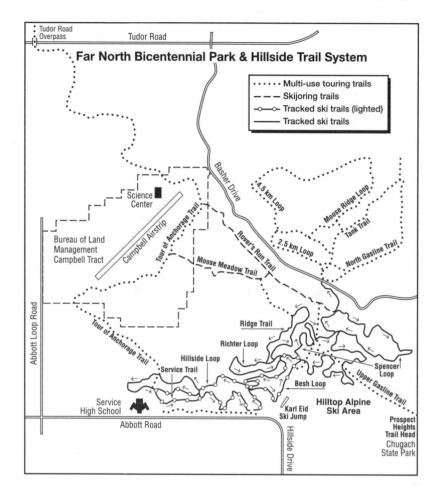

Far North Bicentennial Park & Hillside Trail System

- · · · · · · Multi-use touring trails
- – – – Skijoring trails
- –o–o– Tracked ski trails (lighted)
- ——— Tracked ski trails

by dog mushers and hikers for years, and trail development in the area continued after BLM turned most of the land over to the Municipality of Anchorage as Far North Bicentennial Park in 1976. BLM has retained 730 acres, called the Campbell Tract, for administrative purpose until 2002, when the status of the land will be reviewed.

Today twenty miles of trails run throughout this wilderness park. Not regularly groomed and usually tracked only during the Tour of

Anchorage, these gradual trails are used primarily for touring and skijoring (dogs are welcome). Dog mushers also use some of the trails in winter.

During the summer, the trails are extensively used by horseback riders, mountain bikers, runners, and hikers. Some avid outdoorsmen commute from hillside homes to the University area and midtown offices by bicycle in the summer and ski in the winter. Needless to say, moose and other wildlife use the Bicentennial Park trails both summer and winter. However, because

A FAMILY BUSINESS
Gary King Sporting Goods

Gary King learned to downhill ski with the military troops at Arctic Valley when he was a teenager in Anchorage during World War II. As soon as he finished high school, he began working at Bob Seaman's Sport Shop and teaching skiing to the soldiers at Arctic Valley. He became concerned that the surplus Army skis with cable bindings that his students used were causing frequent leg injuries. He recommended that they instead use the newly developed safety release bindings, which would prevent such injuries.

As a result of his good advice, he was given a contract to supply Elmendorf Air Force Base with about 100 pairs of skis, costing $60 a pair, and $20 release bindings. Initially he sold the skis and bindings out of his living room and at his father-in-law's hardware store on Government Hill.

King's first store opened in 1952 on Fourth Avenue. It only sold ski equipment and was closed in the summer so that he could earn enough money as a house painter to buy inventory for the following winter. Gradually

the area is heavily wooded, moose are not always as evident here as in other places.

Close to the Tour of Anchorage trail where it joins the Old Rondy trail is the park's new Science Center. For more than twenty years, Anchorage schoolchildren have enjoyed Outdoor Week at the BLM's Campbell Tract for hands-on activities in the outdoors. In 1987 the Anchorage Committee for Resource Education, a group of interested educators, parents, and citizens, proposed to build an education complex on the Campbell Tract. Funding was secured through the

King added clothing and equipment for other sports. Now Gary King Sporting Goods stores supply almost every recreational sport except bowling and archery. The main store has shifted locations several times over the years, finally settling on the current Northern Lights Blvd. site in 1980. Branch stores in Wasilla and Girdwood have been added since Gary King's four sons took over the business ten years ago.

All of the King boys grew up skiing and helping with the business. The oldest, Mike, who was a National Alpine Team member and a pioneer freestyle skier, left Alaska in 1995 to start his own business in Spokane, Washington. Gary Jr. is primarily involved now in flying, guiding, and running an allied travel business. Tim is the warehouse manager for Gary King Sporting Goods, and Jim, the youngest, is now the general manager of all the stores.

Although Gary Sr. and his sons ran ski schools at both Arctic Valley and Alyeska for years, they no longer run their own program but provide introductory sessions for area ski schools, to orient new students on use of equipment. Gary King Sr. now lives in Sun Valley, where he is learning to snowboard.

efforts of Senator Ted Stevens, and the day-use building was officially opened on November 2, 1996. At 10,500 square feet, it includes a multi-purpose room, kitchen, classroom, greenhouse, resource library, and caretakers' quarters. The dormitories included in the original proposal have not been built as yet, but are still in the plans. If and when overnight lodging is available, the BLM Science Center could become a spectacular place for out-of-town skiers to stay.

Mahaffey Trails

From Far North Bicentennial Park, the Tour of Anchorage trail crosses a new Tudor Road overpass, completed in 1995 to provide

ELIZABETH TOWER

The covered Tudor Road overpass connects the Bicentennial Park trails with the Mahaffey Trails.

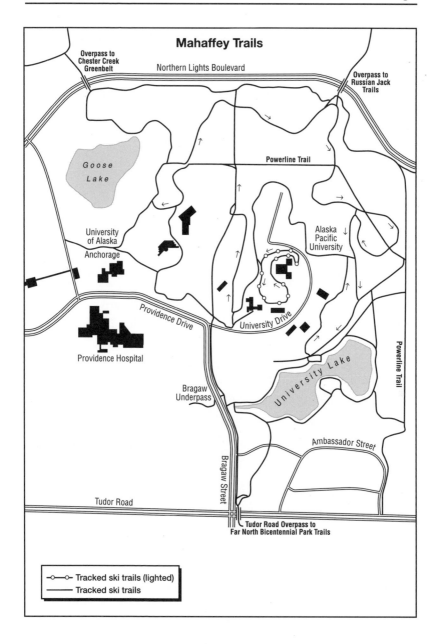

Mahaffey Trails

Overpass to
Chester Creek
Greenbelt

Northern Lights Boulevard

Overpass to
Russian Jack
Trails

*Goose
Lake*

Powerline Trail

University
of Alaska
Anchorage

Alaska
Pacific
University

Providence Drive

University Drive

Providence Hospital

University Lake

Powerline Trail

Bragaw
Underpass

Ambassador Street

Bragaw Street

Tudor Road

Tudor Road Overpass to
Far North Bicentennial Park Trails

—○—○— Tracked ski trails (lighted)
——— Tracked ski trails

skiers with access to the Mahaffey Trails, founded on the campus of Alaska Pacific University. The first 1-kilometer trail at the college, then known as Alaska Methodist University, was designed and built in 1967 by Jim Mahaffey and members of his college ski team. The following year the trail was expanded to 10 kilometers and, in the early 1980s, Mahaffey redesigned the trails to accommodate faster skiing.

Having outgrown Alaska Pacific University, the Mahaffey Trails now also run through the University of Alaska Anchorage campus and wind around University Lake and Goose Lake. These are not as wide as the lighted trails along the Tour of Anchorage, and they have some exciting downhill sections.

Russian Jack Springs Trails

Overpasses crossing Northern Lights Boulevard connect the Mahaffey Trails to Russian Jack Springs Park. Here the Nordic Ski Club developed its first trail in 1963, with the assistance of junior high and high school skiers as part of a summer training program.

Since then, the municipality has developed a ski and sled hill served by a small rope tow, and constructed chalets, which often have been plagued by vandalism. The current chalet serves both the ski area and a nine-hole municipal golf course. A flat, open area adjacent to the chalet is an excellent place for beginners to get their "ski legs."

Through the cooperation of the Nordic Skiing Association of Anchorage and the Municipal Parks and Recreation Department, lights have been installed along the golf course to illuminate the area for night skiing. A 2.5-km loop on the north side of DeBarr Road, developed for intermediate skiers, connects with the 5-km loop through an underpass. The Russian Jack Springs trails are only tracked for diagonal skiing.

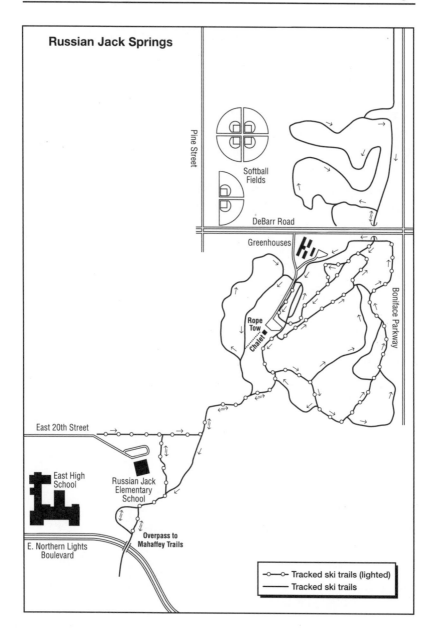

Russian Jack Springs

Pine Street

Softball
Fields

DeBarr Road

Greenhouses

Boniface Parkway

Rope
Tow

Chalet

East 20th Street

East High
School

Russian Jack
Elementary
School

E. Northern Lights
Boulevard

**Overpass to
Mahaffey Trails**

○—○ Tracked ski trails (lighted)
—— Tracked ski trails

Chester Creek and Coastal Multi-Use Trails

From the Russian Jack Springs and Mahaffey Trails, the 10-km Lanie Fleisher Chester Creek Trail leads west, following Chester Creek through a greenbelt area. It connects with the 17-km Tony Knowles Coastal Trail at Westchester Lagoon, which is a popular ice skating area in winter. The Coastal Trail follows the shore of Knik Arm for eight miles south to Kincaid Park and one mile north to downtown Anchorage.

The Municipal Department of Parks and Recreation grooms the trails for both skating and diagonal striding in the winter. Both the Chester Creek and the Coastal trails are relatively flat; in summer

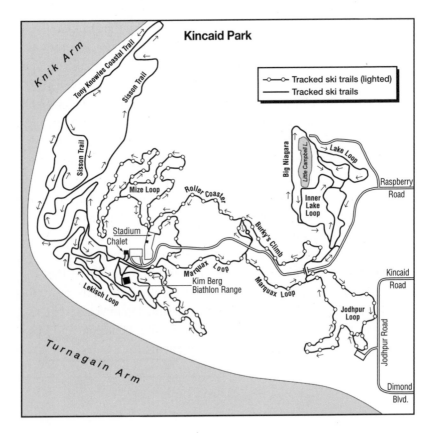

they are paved bicycle trails. Beautiful views of Cook Inlet and downtown Anchorage along the trails attract more than just skiers — dog-walkers, baby-strollers, and walking commuters also frequent them on sunny days. Use courtesy when sharing the trails with others. If accompanied by your dog, keep it on a lead or under voice control. Pooper-scoopers are provided at spots along the trails.

Kincaid Park Trails

The Tour of Anchorage ends at the Kincaid Park stadium, which is well equipped with timing devices and a public address system. At 1,500-acres, Kincaid Park is the site of Anchorage's most extensive system of cross-country ski trails. In 1971 trails in the original park near Little Campbell Lake were first used by the Dimond High School ski team. Dimond ski coaches Dick Mize, Jim Burkholder, and Jon Elliot designed and constructed the first 7.5-km trail around the lake in 1972 and added an additional twelve kilometers in 1974. In 1979 the city acquired the former military site at Point Campbell and added it to the park, more than doubling the available terrain.

Development of the area has continued since 1980, with the addition of eleven kilometers of lighted trail, a stadium and timing building, the Mize Loop, the Lekisch Loop, the Kim Berg Biathlon Range, and the Sisson Trail. These trails vary in difficulty. The Mize Loop and the Sisson Trail are the easiest, while the Lekisch Trails are the most difficult with challenging downhill sections. The Lake Loop trails are narrow and only tracked for diagonal skiing.

Approved by the Federation International de Ski (FIS), the Kincaid Park trails are currently the only internationally homologated (completely surveyed and approved) trails in the United States. Kincaid Park has been the site of Junior, Senior, Biathlon, and Masters World and National cross-country events.

Other Cross-Country Trails

Only one major cross-country ski area is not connected to the Tour of Anchorage trail system — the one at Bartlett High School, 25500 Muldoon, which serves the north side of Anchorage. The school has developed a 5-km trail system, with some lights. Open to the public, its trails are groomed for both skating and classical skiing.

Some of the city's elementary schools also have short trails for their own students, but these are not regularly maintained. Trails on the Moose Run Golf Course, at the base of the Arctic Valley Ski Bowl Road, were the first racing trails in the Anchorage area. The trails on that golf course and the one on Elmendorf Air Force Base, though groomed by the military, can be used by the public.

Cross-Country Ski Instruction

A variety of cross-country skiing lessons are offered for both adults and children in the Anchorage area.

Municipal Cross-Country Ski Lessons: Anchorage Parks and Recreation offers a variety of lessons for those wishing to learn to ski or refresh and enhance their classical skiing skills. Classes are taught on evenings and weekends, at Russian Jack Springs Park and at Kincaid Park. There is usually no charge for these programs, but it may change from year to year. For more information on all municipal winter ski programs, call the Kincaid Park Chalet at 907-343-6397 or Anchorage Parks and Recreation at 907-343-4474. Or pick up a brochure available at both the Kincaid and Russian Jack chalets.

Anchorage Junior Nordic League: One of the hallmarks of this parent-run organization, sponsored by Anchorage Parks and Recreation, is its emphasis on family involvement. More than 500 children and 100 adult volunteers and coaches participate each year. Children between ages six and thirteen learn both classical and skating techniques in practice sessions three times a week on either the

Kincaid or the Hillside trails. Rental skis and jackets are included in the session fee, but members must supply their own boots and poles. For more information, phone the Kincaid Park Chalet at 907-343-6397.

In the Chugiak-Eagle River area, the Bill Koch League runs a similar program for local children at the Beach Lake trails.

Little Nordic Cross-Country Ski Club: Anchorage Parks and Recreation has created a new program for five-year-olds. Participants must provide their own skis, boots, and poles. The location varies from year to year, so call the Kincaid Park Chalet at 907-343-6397 for more information.

Muni-Masters Cross-Country Skiing Group: This training program, offered by Anchorage Parks and Recreation, is designed for adults who wish to improve their physical conditioning and athletic ability; it includes training in both classical and skating techniques. Many students in this program make participation in the Tour of Anchorage Ski Race their personal goal. For information, contact the Kincaid Park Chalet at 907-343-6397 or Anchorage Parks and Recreation at 907-343-4474.

Alaska Sports Academy: This private organization works in partnership with Anchorage Parks and Recreation to offer a winter program in classical and skate-skiing for juniors, seniors, and masters with intermediate to advanced abilities. Sports Academy uses various trails — usually in Kincaid or Hillside Park — depending on snow conditions and the status of the trails. For more information call 907-566-0480 or 907-346-6934.

Recreational Equipment Inc. (REI): The outdoor gear store at 1200 Northern Lights Blvd. offers regular free cross-country skiing clinics, and classes with varying fees during the snow season. Locations vary. For more information, call 907-272-4565.

Alpine Alternatives offers cross-country ski instruction for people with disabilities at Hilltop Ski Area. For information, call 907-561-6655.

Anchorage Community Schools also periodically offer cross-country ski lessons at nominal fees. For information, call 907-269-2450.

UAA Alaska Wilderness Studies Program includes classes in cross-country skiing, telemark skiing, and beginning downhill skiing. Phone 907-786-4066.

Alaska Pacific University has teamed up with REI to offer classes for beginners and intermediates on the Mahaffey Trails. Phone REI at 907-272-4565 or the Alaska Pacific University Mosely Sports Center at 907-564-8314.

Hilltop Ski Area

Downhill skiers in Anchorage who don't want to make the hour-long drive to Mt. Alyeska or Alpenglow can enjoy skiing at the Hilltop Ski Area, in the southeast corner of Far North Bicentennial Park, less than half an hour from downtown Anchorage. Although the 2,090-foot double chair rises only 294 feet, Hilltop's gentle, well-groomed slopes are an ideal place for very young children to be introduced to downhill skiing and for timorous adults to try out new equipment like telemark skis or snowboards. The Hilltop area is well lighted, so after-work skiing is possible at least five nights a week. Youth training programs are held regularly after school.

The Hilltop Ski Area was developed by Hilltop Youth Inc., an organization of original Hillside homesteaders who banded together in 1955 to create recreational opportunities for children growing up on the outskirts of Anchorage. In about 1960, Hilltop Youth acquired equipment for a rope tow from Arctic Valley and set it up on a hill in a gravel pit at the end of Abbott Road, on what was actually still military land. For many years, volunteers ran the little Hilltop rope-tow area and developed the Termite Racing Program there.

When it became evident that the Bicentennial Park land would be turned over to the Municipality of Anchorage in 1976, the Hilltop Youth board began planning to relocate and expand the ski area.

ELIZABETH TOWER

At Hilltop Ski Area, a class of young skiers practices balancing on one ski.

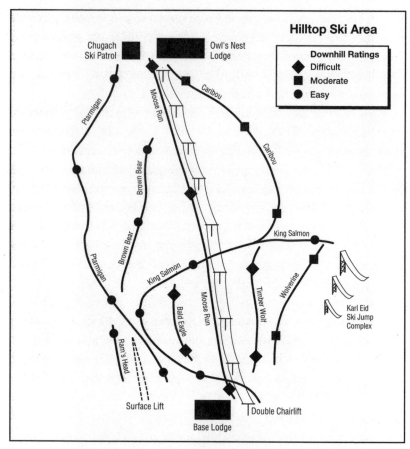

They were fortunate to have conditional approval of their plans when oil revenues started flowing into the State of Alaska in 1980. Hilltop Youth Inc. received a state grant in 1982 to install a chair lift and clear the slopes.

Hilltop Ski Area opened in the winter of 1983-4. Even though that year was blessed with heavy snowfall, so many skiers took advantage of the area that the slopes were scraped bare. The following summer, Hilltop obtained a bank loan to install snowmaking equipment, which has been essential for operation in light snow years. Recently snowboarding has become very popular at Hilltop, accounting for about 40 percent of its business. Total visits by skiers and snowboarders have leveled off at 50,000 per year, which will probably remain constant unless Hilltop can realize its plans to install a longer chair lift and expand on the gradual slopes to the northeast of the current cleared area.

Youth programs continue to be the primary mission of the Hilltop Ski Area. Grants make downhill skiing possible for underprivileged youth and disabled skiers. In 1991, Hilltop hired a well-qualified coach and the Termite Racing Program evolved into SPYDER, which stands for Ski Program for Youth Development, Education, and Recreation. Night skiing at Hilltop enables young racers to train diligently and compete successfully with Mighty Mites from the larger downhill ski areas. Roger Head, who has been instrumental in Hilltop development, contends that learning to pick up speed on the gentle Hilltop slopes facilitates good downhill racing on steeper hills.

Hilltop is open Wednesday through Sunday and all school holidays for day and night skiing. It provides food service, ski school, and a rental shop. The administrative office at 907-346-1446 can provide more information. For a ski report, phone 907-346-2167.

SPOTLIGHT: Ski Jumping

Ski jumping is no longer as popular a sport as it was when Scandinavians brought it to Alaska in the early twentieth century — probably because Alaska now offers so many other skiing activities to choose from. Before World War II, the ski jump in the Anchorage Ski Bowl at the end of Fourth Avenue was the center of skiing activity, and the leading jumpers were town heroes. After that jump was dismantled, jumps at Russian Jack Springs, Alaska Pacific University, and Alyeska were used briefly and then demolished because of concern for potential liability.

In 1979 Karl Eid, a German ski jumper who had moved to Anchorage in 1959, worked with local nordic skiers John Cress and

Tobben Spurkland to plan a 60-meter jump. They received a $25,000 grant from the Alaska State Legislature and, after studying potential sites, they selected one adjacent to the Hilltop Ski Area in Far North Bicentennial Park. Using volunteer labor, the Nordic Skiing Association of Anchorage erected 15-m and 30-m jumps that had natural outruns and prepared a landing area for a 60-m jump.

When Far North Bicentennial Park became municipal property in 1985, the Municipality of Anchorage and Alaska State Legislature dedicated the ski jumping facility as the Karl Eid Jump Complex. The inrun tower for the 60-meter jump was constructed in 1988 with private funds and dedicated to the memory of Jim Landes, an avid alpine skier and ski jumper.

The Karl Eid Jump Complex currently is the only active ski jumping facility in Alaska; jumps no longer exist in Fairbanks or Juneau. The Jumping Committee of the Nordic Skiing Association of Anchorage runs an active jumping program for up to forty jumpers, and the United States Ski Association sanctions both a jumping and a nordic combined (cross-country racing plus jumping) series.

SPOTLIGHT: Skijoring

When my family started cross-country skiing in Anchorage thirty-five years ago, one of our greatest pleasures was the companionship of our dog and the obvious delight he took in running on the trails. We saw rescue dogs being trained in Norway in 1970 and brought back a leather harness for our husky. Our twelve-year-old son loved tearing around the Russian Jack ski trails behind the dog for a year or two, and we enjoyed having dogs with us when we skied, even if they weren't pulling us. But as trail grooming became more sophisticated, our dogs were no longer welcome on the trails.

In recent years, the Scandinavian sport of skijoring has become popular in the Anchorage area, and dogs are becoming active participants rather than just fellow travelers. Dogs are still forbidden

ELIZABETH TOWER

A joring dog does double-duty, pulling its owner and her baby along the Tony Knowles Coastal Trail.

on tracked trails reserved for cross-country skiing, but they are welcome on the 17-km Tony Knowles Coastal Trail, on the 10-km Chester Creek Greenbelt Multi-Use Trail, and on some of the Mahaffey Trails in the University area. Also, some trails have been developed specifically for skijoring, including fifteen kilometers at Connors Lake, at the corner of Jewel Lake Road and International Airport Road, and twenty kilometers in Far North Bicentennial Park.

Dogs of almost any breed, weighing between forty and sixty-five pounds, can be trained to pull a skier. Some of the best joring dogs can be obtained at the municipal dog pound. Rae's Harness Shop on Dowling Road in Anchorage carries specialized joring equipment and invites dogs in for a personal harness fitting. Other stores that carry sled dog supplies often have joring equipment as well.

The North American Skijor and Ski-Pulk Association (NASSPA) holds free beginners' clinics at Connors Lake to help novices understand this new sport. It also holds regularly scheduled races at various locations. Joring trails are groomed by NASSPA volunteers, and all except Rover's Run in Bicentennial Park are wide enough for skate-skiing.

Skijoring is also popular in other areas throughout the state, particularly around Fairbanks, where the North American Skijor and Ski-Pulk Association holds races up to fifty kilometers long.

Carol Kaynor and Mari Hoe-Raito have recently published *Skijor With Your Dog*, the first comprehensive, full-length book on skijoring. It is available through OK Publishing, P.O. Box 84302, Fairbanks, AK 99708-4302.

For more information about skijoring in the Anchorage area, call the local chapter of the NASSPA at 907-349-WOOF.

SPOTLIGHT: Biathlon

Biathlon, the Olympic sport that combines target shooting with cross-country skiing, was introduced to Alaskans in 1958 when Fort Richardson on the outskirts of Anchorage was selected to be the U.S. Army Biathlon Training Center.

While biathletes were still stationed at Fort Richardson, the Nordic Ski Club, the United States Ski Association (USSA), and

ELIZABETH TOWER

At the Kincaid Outdoor Center, biathletes take aim during the 1996 Arctic Winter Games.

the Anchorage School District were permitted to use the ten kilometers of Army biathlon trails off Arctic Valley Ski Bowl Road to hold races for local residents and high school students. Some former soldiers with biathlon experience later retired in Alaska and continued to support the sport. Ken Alligood, one of the early Anchorage high school skiers, has become an international biathlon competitor and coach.

After the Army Biathlon Center moved from Fort Richardson, Alaska was without a biathlon range until the Kincaid Outdoor Center was turned over to Anchorage Parks and Recreation in 1986. At the twenty-two-target biathlon range adjacent to the Andrew Lekisch Memorial Trail, Kincaid Park hosted the U.S. Biathlon Championships and the North American Biathlon Championships in 1992, the U.S. Biathlon Olympic Tryout Races in 1993, and the Arctic Winter Games biathlon races in 1996.

In Fairbanks, Fort Wainwright maintains a biathlon range in conjunction with the Birch Hill Recreation Area cross-country trails. Small ranges also have been developed near the Skyview High School trails in Soldotna and the Mineral Creek trails in Valdez.

Biathlon continues to grow as a sport in Alaska, with both male and female competitors. A group of young biathletes from Southcentral Alaska had a very successful competitive year in 1996-97. Jay Poss and Jeremy Teela from Anchorage and Jay Hakkinen from Soldotna took three of the four spots on the U.S. Men's World Championship biathlon team by dominating the national championships. Poss became the first Alaskan to win a national biathlon title since the 1980s, while Hakkinen and Teela both had top-five finishes in two races. Hakkinen, at age nineteen, was the top American at the World Championships and then became the first American to win a gold medal at the World Junior Championship. Rachel Steer of Anchorage, age nineteen, won silver and bronze medals at the World University Games.

Information on the Alaska Biathlon Association can be obtained by calling the Kincaid Outdoor Center at 907-343-6397. For information on the Fairbanks Biathlon Club, write to P.O. Box 81821, Fairbanks, AK 99708.

WARNING: Beware of Birds and Beasts

Cross-country skiers in the Anchorage area soon realize that they are sharing their kilometers of groomed ski trails with a sizable cadre of urban moose. Although not the most intelligent of animals, moose understand that packed trails are much easier to get around on than three feet of unpacked snow.

Moose and skiers have established a code for sharing the trails — one in which the moose are given the right-of-way. Some skiers, made confident by their years of experience with moose, refuse to break stride and ski right by the animals. A wiser decision, however, is to do a 180-degree turn and ski in the opposite direction. Although moose do not usually attack or even pursue skiers, one moose attack at Kincaid Park in Anchorage during the 1996-7 season did result in minor injuries to a skier. Moose have occasionally turned up as spectators at cross-country ski races, which sometimes have been canceled or postponed until patrolling snow machines could persuade the moose to retreat.

Several years ago, another formidable animal began to harass skiers on Anchorage trails. On a chilly January night in 1989, a lone skier was attacked by an owl, which apparently mistook his gray pile ski hat for a rabbit.

"I was going down a long hill and felt this thing hit me on the back of the head," he recalled. "As I looked behind, I saw these rather large wings. I felt this tightening around my scalp and reached up and grabbed the legs of a full-grown great horned owl."

While attempting to retrieve his hat, the skier also lost his glove. He escaped for a moment, but about forty feet down the trail he felt the talons imbedded in his back. Several other skiers, hearing his call for help, assisted him in removing his jacket, vest, and T-shirt, which were all attached to the owl's talons. With the temperature at five below zero, the victim found himself stripped to the waist. Passing skiers loaned him enough clothing to ski two miles back to the Kincaid recreational center.

CAROLYN STRAND

On the Mize Loop in Kincaid Park, a young moose contests right of way with two cross-country skiers.

The owl escaped unharmed — which was fortunate for the skier. Killing a great horned owl carries a maximum fine of $5,000 and a jail term of six months. One U.S. Fish and Wildlife agent said, however, that in this case a judge probably would have considered the extenuating circumstances.

Several years later an owl struck again, this time at the Hilltop Ski Area. At least three skiers and snowboarders lost their hats to an owl while skiing at night. Numerous attempts to trap the owl, including baiting a trap with a little girl's pet bunny, were of no avail until a local home-owner caught an owl attacking his pet ducks. The owl was transported to an uninhabited area miles away, and the attacks on skiers ceased.

The moral of this story is to avoid wearing any clothing that might be mistaken for a rabbit when skiing in a wooded area at night.

A telemarker leaves the Glen Alps trailhead on one of the many ski loops in Chugach State Park near Anchorage.

2. OUTSIDE ANCHORAGE

Skiers willing to make an hour-long or half-hour drive from downtown Anchorage will find a variety of opportunities just outside the city, in the nearby Chugach Mountains to the east. Chugach State Park, accessible from trailheads inside and outside Anchorage, is the third largest state park in the nation, offering trails through forests, lakes, mountains, and valleys. A short drive northeast from Anchorage on the Glenn Highway takes skiers to Alpenglow in Arctic Valley, Alaska's oldest downhill skiing area. Driving southeast on the Seward Highway along scenic Turnagain Arm, skiers find their way to Alaska's largest and most complete alpine skiing resort at Mt. Alyeska.

Chugach State Park

In the foothills and mountains behind Anchorage, 495,000-acre Chugach State Park provides skiers with unlimited possibilities for touring and telemarking. An extensive trail system has been developed in the park, but these trails are not as meticulously groomed as those in Anchorage. Trailheads with parking lots at Glen Alps, Upper Huffman, O'Malley, and Prospect Heights provide easy access to the loop trails of the Chugach Park Hillside Trail System; maps are posted at the trailheads. These scenic loop trails, at or above treeline, give skiers spectacular views of the city and the mountain ranges surrounding it. Since dogs are allowed on these trails, they are often brought here to exercise with their skiing owners.

ELIZABETH TOWER

Wolverine Peak, in Chugach State Park, is a popular destination for skiers.

One popular though partially unmaintained course, the 14-mi. Wolverine Loop, starts and ends at the Prospect Heights trailhead. It leads east through the pass under Near Point and to Long Lake, then around the base of Wolverine Peak and back west through the Williwaw Lakes. This loop through beautiful alpine countryside is fairly safe from avalanches, but the passes below Wolverine Peak can be hazardous, particularly just after a heavy snowstorm.

Every March, the University of Alaska Anchorage ski team launches its annual race, known as the Flattop Flyer, from the Glen Alps trailhead. The 12-km race leads over the loop trails and an unmaintained trail connecting Prospect Heights to the Hillside Park Trail System, ending at Service High School. A long downhill run with some steep pitches, sharp turns, and jumps, the Flattop Flyer

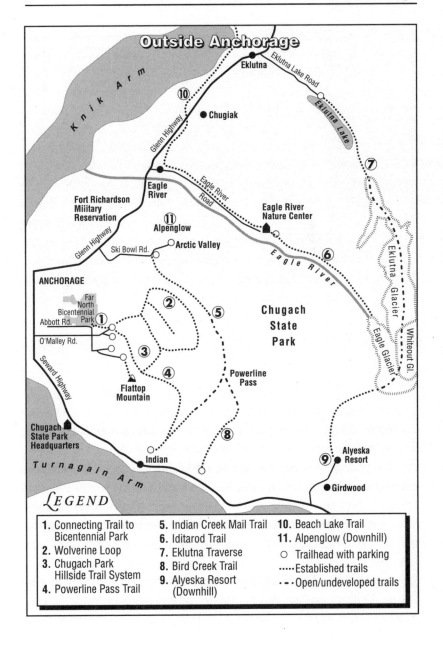

Outside Anchorage

LEGEND

1. Connecting Trail to Bicentennial Park
2. Wolverine Loop
3. Chugach Park Hillside Trail System
4. Powerline Pass Trail
5. Indian Creek Mail Trail
6. Iditarod Trail
7. Eklutna Traverse
8. Bird Creek Trail
9. Alyeska Resort (Downhill)
10. Beach Lake Trail
11. Alpenglow (Downhill)
○ Trailhead with parking
····· Established trails
· - · Open/undeveloped trails

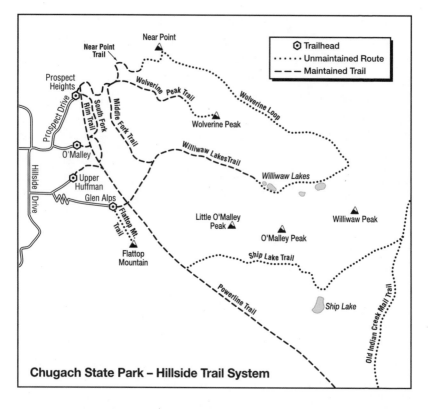

Chugach State Park – Hillside Trail System

has been called "the wildest ride on cross-country skis around." Trees and poles that are potentially hazardous are padded with mattresses, and all competitors are required to wear bicycle helmets. So far no serious injuries have occurred in the three years that the race has been run. Some skiers have tried using telemark skis with steel edges for more control, but since there are some flat and slightly uphill sections, cross-country racing skis have been the most successful.

Another popular adventure in spring is the 20-mi. tour from the Arctic Valley Road to Indian, following the historic Indian Creek Mail Trail (also called the Ship Creek Trail). This longer route circles numerous mountains and offers beautiful views of Anchorage,

Turnagain Arm, and Knik Arm. From Mile 6 on Arctic Valley Ski Bowl Road, the circuit leads up Ship Creek Valley and along the south fork of Ship Creek to Ship Lake. Skiers then head northeast up a steep slope, and down a gentle valley into the south fork of Campbell Creek. From there you can either come out at Glenn Alps, follow the Powerline Trail to Prospect Heights, or continue south through Bird Creek Pass or Indian Creek Pass (both of which are susceptible to avalanches).

The entire Old Mail Trail tour to Indian on the Seward Highway can usually be done in one day in late March or April when the days are long enough. Currently there are no shelters on this trail, although there were years ago before the Alaska Railroad and the Seward Highway were built. Mail was historically brought to Cook Inlet settlements via this trail because the avalanche danger was not as great as on the Iditarod Trail from Girdwood to Eagle River.

A flat portion of that historic trail can be safely used for skiing, starting at the nonprofit Eagle River Nature Center (phone 907-694-2108) at the end of Eagle River Road. If it's cold enough and late enough in the year, skiers may find good touring along the frozen river, with good snow cover. Continuing through the Eagle River Valley, it's 14.6 miles to Eagle Lake and farther to Eagle Glacier. The full stretch of the Iditarod Trail leads twenty-six miles to Crow Creek Road outside of Girdwood, but it is not recommended because the Girdwood portion of the trail passes through steep terrain where avalanches may occur. The Mountaineering Club of Alaska maintains a shelter at Crow Pass.

One extremely remote and challenging tour is the Eklutna Traverse, a 32-mi. trip mostly over glaciers. From Crow Creek Road out of Girdwood, the traverse leads north up the ridge toward Goat Mountain and over Eagle Glacier, crosses a crevassed area to White-out Glacier (the largest glacier in the park at more than forty square miles), then continues north to Eklutna Glacier and Eklutna Lake. Only those experienced at glacier touring — and glacier rescue techniques — should attempt it, and it is used more by mountaineers than ski tourers. A good source of information about the Eklutna Traverse, therefore, is the Mountaineering Club of Alaska, reachable at P.O. Box 2037, Anchorage, AK 99510. An exception to the high difficulty and danger levels of the traverse is the area immediately around Eklutna Lake, which the park service recommends as safe even for beginning skiers.

The nearby slopes in the state park are frequently used by Anchorage telemark skiers and snowboarders when snow conditions are favorable. In a gully between O'Malley Peak and Little O'Malley Peak, for instance, I enjoyed some of the best telemark skiing I have ever experienced. The back side of Flattop Mountain also can be good for telemarking, but is prone to avalanches. Several local skiers were killed in an avalanche on these slopes in 1993. For information about potential avalanche hazard, call the Avalanche Hotline at 907-273-6037.

For more information about trails in Chugach State Park, contact the Alaska Division of Parks and Outdoor Recreation, Pouch 10-7001, Anchorage, AK 99510, phone 907-762-2617, or the Chugach State Park Headquarters, HC 52, Box 8999, Indian, AK 99540, phone 907-345-5014. Or visit the Chugach State Park Headquarters at Mile 115 of the Seward Highway. For a twenty-four-hour Chugach State Park Recreation Report, phone 907-694-6391.

Detailed information on backcountry skiing in the Chugach Mountains and elsewhere can be found in the book *Skiing Alaska's Back Forty*, a joint publication of Alaska Wilderness Treks, the Anchorage Nordic Ski Patrol, and Glacier House Productions (Box 201901, Anchorage, AK 99520).

Alpenglow Ski Area at Arctic Valley

A thirty-minute drive from downtown Anchorage takes skiers to Alpenglow, the alpine ski area at Arctic Valley. From near the Fort Richardson gate, seven miles north of Anchorage along the

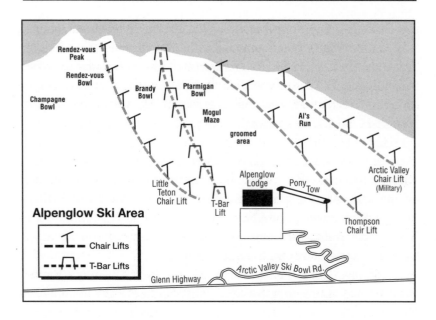

Rendez-vous Peak

Rendez-vous Bowl

Champagne Bowl

Brandy Bowl

Ptarmigan Bowl

Mogul Maze

groomed area

Al's Run

Little Teton Chair Lift

T-Bar Lift

Alpenglow Lodge

Pony Tow

Arctic Valley Chair Lift (Military)

Thompson Chair Lift

Alpenglow Ski Area

Chair Lifts

T-Bar Lifts

Glenn Highway

Arctic Valley Ski Bowl Rd.

Glenn Highway, Arctic Valley Ski Bowl Road runs another seven miles up into the Chugach Mountains. Along the way, pullouts provide views of the city and the McKinley Range. From a base elevation of 2,500 feet, Alpenglow's lifts rise to almost 4,000 feet, providing skiers with almost a mile of varied, open slopes.

Alpenglow is Southcentral Alaska's oldest alpine ski area, developed in part by the Anchorage Ski Club. The club was organized in January 1937 by twenty-one skiing enthusiasts, who met in the Richmond Cafe on a Sunday afternoon to plan Anchorage's first ski tournament, discuss special classes for youngsters, and study the potential for skiing in the Chugach Mountains east of the city.

Initially, however, the Anchorage Ski Club focused on developing a slope overlooking Ship Creek in downtown Anchorage, a site which eventually was equipped with a rope tow and a ski jump. The City Ski Bowl served the Anchorage area until the Alaska Native Health Service hospital was built on the site in 1952.

Even before the closure of the old City Ski Bowl, the Anchorage

Ski Club started shifting its attention back to the Chugach Mountains, where the military had developed a ski area during World War II. Back in 1941, Col. M. R. ("Muktuk") Marston arrived in the Anchorage area as a U.S. Air Force major with special services in charge of recreation. His mandate was to "do something for the morale of the GIs in Alaska."

Before Marston arrived, Russell Dow, a former Dartmouth skier, had been training Army ski troops on the City Ski Bowl slopes. Muktuk and his staff — which included Bob Thompson, a member of the elite Alaska scouts known as "Castner's Cutthroats" — searched the country for a hundred miles around Anchorage for a better ski training area and selected the Arctic Valley site in the Chugach Mountains overlooking Anchorage.

The new ski area was developed and operated jointly by the military and Anchorage Ski Club members until the late 1940s. When civilian skiers became so numerous that there wasn't enough room in the military warm-up building, the Anchorage Ski Club moved up the valley and built its own lodge and rope tows. Bob Thompson, who had settled in Anchorage and become a leader in the development of the ski facilities, was killed during a summer work party in 1954. The hill above the lodge has been named in his honor.

As the ski club membership grew, it became evident that the three long rope tows were not sufficient to meet the demand. Planning for the purchase of a T-bar lift started in 1959, with money raised through the sale of life memberships. Volunteers excavated ground for installation of the towers. The T-bar lift, which replaced a long rope tow with a 984-foot vertical rise, was dedicated on December 15, 1961 — a day when the temperature registered 20 degrees below zero.

In 1969, the rope tow that rose 813 vertical feet was replaced with the Thompson double chairlift. The addition of the Little Teton chairlift more than doubled the lift-accessible ski area in 1977.

Meanwhile, the military also replaced its rope tow with a double chairlift.

The old civilian warm-up hut and outdoor privies were replaced in 1972 by a two-story ski lodge with running water, indoor plumbing, heated restrooms, a snack bar, and picture windows overlooking the slopes. Road improvements and the advent of cars with front-wheel drive and studded tires have greatly improved the accessibility of this scenic ski area overlooking Anchorage.

The Arctic Valley ski slopes are still jointly owned and operated by the U.S. Army special services at Fort Richardson and the Anchorage Ski Club. Although the name Alpenglow refers to the Anchorage Ski Club facilities, civilian skiers and snowboarders also can use the military lifts and slopes. Entirely above treeline, the ski area's facilities now include three chairlifts, a T-bar/Platter lift, and several rope tows. Both sides of the area are equipped with lights for night skiing.

Since the ski area does not have snowmaking capabilities, conditions are dependent on the weather. Although partially shielded on the north by Mt. Gordon Lyon, some of the slopes can be affected by crosswinds that leave the snow unevenly distributed. Grooming is only attempted on some of the gradual runs, so acres of untracked snow are available on the steeper slopes for dedicated powder skiers and telemarkers who arrive at Alpenglow after a new snow before the wind blows. There are rarely any lift lines when all the lifts are running because the area could potentially accommodate 4,000 skiers per hour. However, some of the aging equipment has not run reliably during the past several ski seasons.

Alpenglow Ski Area is open for day and night skiing from Wednesday through Sunday. The rental shop offers downhill skis, boots, poles, and snowboards. Its ski school, which is staffed by instructors certified by the Professional Ski Instructors of America, provides snowboard and telemark instruction as well as downhill classes for all skill levels. Discounts are available for members of the Anchorage Ski Club. For more information, call the Alpenglow office at 907-563-2524, the lodge at 907-428-1208, or the hotline at 907-249-9292.

Beach Lake Trails

Twenty miles northeast of downtown Anchorage on the Glenn Highway is the 15-km Beach Lake cross-country trail system, adjacent to Chugiak High School. Although the Chugiak-Eagle River area is technically part of the Municipality of Anchorage, this ski area was developed and is maintained by the Eagle River Nordic Ski Club.

Residents of the area organized the club in the 1970s to provide community support for cross-country skiers of all ages and ability levels. When the Chugiak-Eagle River community hosted the Arctic Winter Games in March 1996, the Beach Lake Trails were used not only by Alaskans but by competitors from Yukon Territory, Northwest Territory, Northern Alberta, Greenland, and the Russian Far East.

The Eagle River Nordic Ski Club grooms the Beach Lake Trails for both skating and diagonal skiing, and maintains lighting on four kilometers of trail. It also runs a Junior Nordic program, including

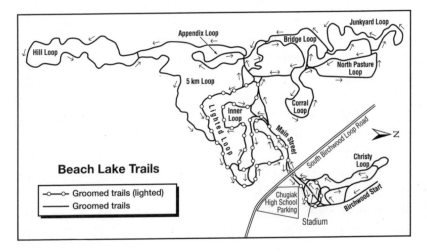

ELIZABETH TOWER

Racers emerge from tunnels on the Beach Lake Trails near Chugiak during the 1996 Arctic Winter Games.

ski instruction and recreational races for elementary school through junior high school age youth, and organizes ski tours, usually on weekends, to various locations in Southcentral Alaska. For more information, call the Eagle River Nordic Ski Club at 907-694-2597.

Alyeska Resort

Tommy Moe's victories at the 1994 Olympics brought international recognition to his home training ground at Alyeska, Alaska's largest and most complete alpine ski area. The resort is in the Chugach Range at the old mining village of Girdwood, a forty-mile drive southeast from downtown Anchorage on the Seward Highway along Turnagain Arm, a fjord between rugged snowcapped mountains.

Due to Alyeska's base elevation of only 260 feet above sea level and the moderating effect of the Japanese current, winter temperatures are mild, averaging 10 to 30 degrees Fahrenheit. Snowfall at Alyeska averages 560 inches annually. The ski season lasts from November through April; Alyeska usually closes the ski area in mid-April to prepare for the summer tourist season. After school lets out in early June, there is still adequate snow on the glacier above the tramway terminal to hold camps for aspiring young alpine racers. The tramway runs all summer to serve the Seven Glaciers restaurant and treat tourists to an excellent view of Turnagain Arm.

Nine lifts — one high-speed detachable quad, two fixed-grip quads, three double chairs, two pony lifts, and one sixty-passenger aerial tram — serve 225 acres of trails with a vertical rise of 2,500 feet. Almost three-quarters of the sixty-two runs are classed as intermediate, with the remainder divided between expert and beginner. Additional expert runs were made available to skiers during the 1996-7 season, when the steep north face of the mountain was opened.

Snow conditions vary considerably over the mountain, which stretches from sea level to almost 4,000 feet, providing ample challenge to skiers. Most of the main trails are well groomed. Snowmaking is available on eighteen trails, covering 12 percent of the total acreage. Since daylight is short in mid-winter, averaging seven hours in December, night skiing is popular on more than 2,000 feet of vertical terrain.

ELIZABETH TOWER

A tramway carries passengers up Alyeska's steep north face for downhill skiing or an elegant meal at the Seven Glaciers restaurant.

Although the Japanese-owned Seibu Alaska, Inc. now manages the Alyeska Resort, initial marketing of the area was pioneered by Alaskan ski buffs Bob Bursiel, Sven Johanssen, and Ernie Bauman, who skied the area by helicopter and light plane, and recognized Mt. Alyeska as one of the best mountains anywhere for skiing. They engaged Frances Richins Clark of Anchorage to find potential investors to finance the construction of lifts, and she located Francois deGunsburg, who had traveled to Alaska frequently as an oil lease broker.

"Frenchy" deGunsburg convinced his Owanah Oil Company to invest in the first phase of development, which included a 1,250-foot Pomalift, clearing of ski trails, and construction of a small lodge and manager's living quarters. The grand opening in December 1959 was delayed for several weeks due to lack of snow. The first chairlift and day lodge were built in 1960, but the small local market was not sufficient to make the development profitable initially. Jim Branch, the first manager, spent much of his time maintaining the winding, gravel road and homemade bridges that were the only access to Alyeska from the Seward Highway.

Although deGunsburg had to subsidize the operation in the early years, in time the resort was discovered by foreign skiers, employees of airlines that used Anchorage as a refueling base. They spread the word about the resort, and for many years Alyeska was the site of the International Airline Races. Riding the Alyeska chairlift in those days was an international experience; Japanese lift companions often took advantage of the opportunity to practice their English.

In 1967 deGunsburg decided to sell the resort and entered into a three-year management contract with Alaska Airlines with an option to purchase. Chris von Imhof, director of tourism for the State of Alaska, who had skied at Alyeska and was impressed with its potential, agreed to become general manager of the resort. Construction of a seventy-five-room hotel was begun in 1968. The following year condominium units were built and sold privately.

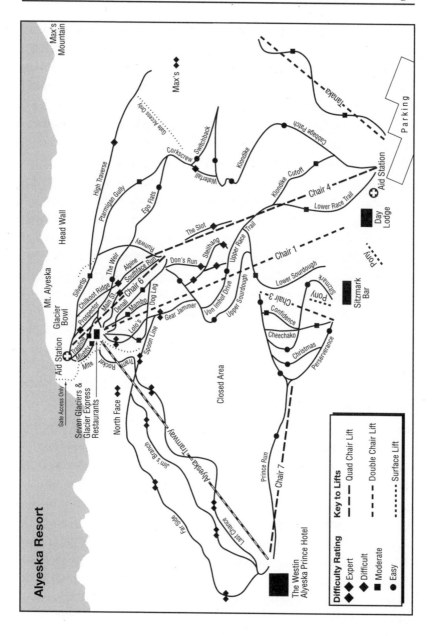

Alyeska Resort

ELIZABETH TOWER

Opened in 1994, the 307-room, chateau-style Alyeska Prince Hotel is the centerpiece of Alyeska Resort.

As Alyeska became more popular, longer lift lines put pressure on the resort to construct a second chairlift. The popular Chairlift No. 2, constructed in 1972, served the upper portion of the mountain, opening skiing terrain with reliably good snow conditions. Chairlift No. 3 was added at the base of the mountain in 1974 to provide more area for beginners. Two years later, Chair No. 4 was built to back up the original lift. Both summer and winter markets increased during the 1970s, and Alaska Airlines decided to sell the resort at a profit rather than face the expense of further development.

In October 1980 Alaska Airlines concluded the sale of Alyeska

ALASKA'S FLYING FISH

Alaska skiing received one of the biggest boosts in its history in 1994 when Tommy Moe from Girdwood brought home two medals from the 1994 Winter Olympics.

Tommy Moe had been a promising young skier when he arrived in Alaska as a thirteen-year-old hot shot in need of discipline. His father enrolled him at the Glacier Creek Academy in Girdwood, where he could study for half the day and train at Mt. Alyeska the rest of the time. Tommy and his friend Darren Mattingly took pride in skiing all the extreme runs on Alyeska. (Mattingly has since placed well in the World Extreme Ski Championships at Valdez.)

At age fifteen Moe won national recognition by finishing sixth in the U.S. National Championship downhill. He competed in his first World Cup downhill at age seventeen. But the glory he expected to find at the 1992 Olympics didn't come. For a while he was regularly beaten by his teammates.

Moe was having a hard time finding financial support when the Alaska Seafood Marketing Institute stepped forward to sponsor him as "Alaska's flying fish." Wearing a fish decal on his helmet, Moe went to the 1994 Olympic Winter Games, winning a gold medal in the downhill and a silver medal in the super-G.

After his Olympic victories, Moe sustained a knee injury. His recovery has been slow, but in the 1996 U.S. Championships he reached the winners' podium again with third place finishes in both downhill and super-G. In 1997 he claimed both the National Downhill and Super-G Championships. Moe has been followed closely by another Glacier Creek Academy alumnus, Mike Makar of Anchorage, who in 1997 placed fifth in the U.S. National Downhill and in the top ten at the U.S. National Super-G. Barring more injuries, both of these Alaska skiers will compete in the 1998 Olympics in Japan.

Resort to the Seibu Group, a Japanese conglomerate with the financial strength, experience, and commitment to develop it into a first-class, year-round resort. Chris von Imhof, who had been managing property for Seibu in Hawaii, returned to Alaska as manager of the Alyeska Resort in 1995.

The centerpiece of the Seibu Group's expansion of Alyeska is the 307-room, chateau-style Alyeska Prince Hotel, which opened on August 26, 1994. As the result of a partnership between Seibu Alaska, Inc. and Westin Hotels and Resorts, skiers can make reservations at the Alyeska Prince Hotel through Westin's central reservation system; guests also receive increased benefits through Westin's frequent guest program and a multitude of frequent flier partnerships. Alyeska Resort offers many guest packages which combine skiing, lodging, and the use of a fitness center and swimming pool.

In addition to the hotel, a day lodge built in 1989 houses food service, a complete rental shop, and a ski school. In the upper tram terminal are located the Glacier Express self-service restaurant and the Seven Glaciers, a fine dining room and lounge featuring panoramic views of Turnagain Arm and the surrounding mountains.

Through the years Alyeska has hosted various major ski events, including the 1964 Olympic Trials, the 1969 Junior Nationals, a 1973 World Cup Giant Slalom, the 1987 World Masters Competition, the 1993 World Junior Olympic Competition, and the 1995 and 1997 U.S. Alpine Masters Championship.

Alyeska is open daily, with night skiing on weekends and holidays from December through March. Shops at both the hotel and the day lodge rent skis, boots, and snowboards and also can repair equipment. The hotel shop also rents cross-country skis and snowshoes. Meadows near the hotel have fifty kilometers of cross-country trails that are usually untracked. Alyeska Resort also coordinates with Chugach Powder Guides and ERA Helicopters to offer heli-skiing in the surrounding Chugach Mountains.

The Alyeska Ski School, operating out of the day lodge, offers classes for skiers of all abilities, as well as snowboard and telemark instruction. Volunteers run an active Mighty Mite racing program for children on weekends.

For more information about Alyeska, write: Alyeska Resort, P.O. Box 249, Girdwood, AK 99587. Phone the resort at 907-754-1111 or the Westin Hotels reservation line at 800-880-3880. For Alyeska's Ski Hotline, call 907-SKI-SNOW.

Summer Glacier Skiing at Eagle Camp

Serious skiing addicts who would rather continue to ski than fish or play golf during the summer don't have to travel to the Andes or New Zealand anymore! Coach Jim Galanes and the Alaska Gold 2002 nordic training program hold several seven-day training camps at the Eagle Glacier Nordic Center during April, May, and June. After skiing at the center during the 1996 season, U.S. Ski Team members expressed their satisfaction, proclaiming it one of the best glacier skiing facilities in the world.

Eagle Camp, as it is known locally, is perched on a high alpine ridge 5,700 feet above Girdwood, its lodge just a few steps from the uppermost portion of Eagle Glacier. More like a snowfield than an icefield, the gently sloping glacier terrain is generally free of crevasses or slides, which makes it ideal for groomed track skiing and ski touring. The view from the camp is expansive, with the 7,000-foot peaks of the Chugach Mountains ringing the glacier. In the opposite direction, the rock massif falls away thousands of feet to the headwaters of Glacier Creek, which flows through Girdwood and into Turnagain Arm. From this height, skiers frequently look down on mountain goats and other wildlife.

Guests of the camp are transported from the Girdwood airport to the glacier airstrip on board a Cessna 185 ski plane by Alpine Air Inc. A Pisten Bully 200 snowcat, which also grooms skating and classical tracks, carries skiers from the airstrip to the lodge.

Bunk-style sleeping quarters with full bedding provided can accommodate groups of up to twenty-five people. The lodge also features a full commercial kitchen, living area, recreation room, sauna, indoor restrooms and showers, stereo system, television, and local phone access via a unique radio phone system.

The center's management, Eagle Glacier Nordic Center Inc., is a nonprofit Alaskan corporation dedicated to providing nordic and biathlon training opportunities for the benefit of United States athletes. Interested training and racing programs are invited to reserve time on the glacier. Nordic skiers can organize tour groups for this spectacular experience, which can be enjoyed by skiers of all skill levels. Special group rates are available for as little as $30 per person per day and $95 per person for round-trip airfare. Chris Nyman, director of the Eagle Glacier Nordic Center, is willing to put together special tour packages upon request. He can be contacted at 907-279-2447. More information is also available on the Internet at eaglegla@alaska.net.

WARNING: Hypothermia

More than thirty years ago, several puzzling incidents occurred in the Chugach Mountains behind Anchorage. The first involved soldiers participating in a training exercise who could not keep up with the rest. Left behind with camping equipment, they were found dead in their sleeping bags the next morning. Several years later, two students on an overnight trip to a cabin near Eklutna Glacier apparently went hiking during the night and were found dead in the morning.

Another episode took place during a sudden snowstorm in early May near Girdwood. Two hikers, clad only in street clothes, were seen wandering aimlessly about by another party of hikers. Although instructed to follow the other hikers, who also were having trouble keeping warm, the two men wandered off and were found dead the following day.

These deaths may well have been caused by hypothermia, an ever-present danger in Alaska, especially in the spring when sudden storms may trap the unprepared hiker or skier. Hypothermia, or cooling of the body temperature, can occur any time of year, usually when temperatures are relatively warm by Alaska standards, between 30 and 50 degrees Fahrenheit. People going out in such weather often fail to bring warmer clothing, then become wet or have to face strong winds. Once chilled, their brains lose the ability to function, leading to poor judgment. Hypothermia victims often cannot help themselves reach warmth or safety. The results are often fatal.

To prevent hypothermia, skiers on tours should dress in layers — wind- and water-resistant outer layers, and inner layers of wool or synthetics that stay warm when wet. A hat may be the most important piece of clothing to prevent heat loss. It's also important to stay well fueled by eating high carbohydrate snacks and to drink lots of water or warm beverages.

By touring in groups, skiers can watch each other for early signs of hypothermia, such as shivering, fatigue, stumbling, poor coordination, slurred speech, or irrationality. Awareness of the early signs of hypothermia is essential because the ensuing confusion, bravado, and lack of judgment can have fatal consequences. Victims of hypothermia are often found to have discarded needed clothing while under the delusion that they are too warm.

A victim of hypothermia should be sheltered from the wind and weather. Wet clothing should be removed and the victim placed in dry clothes or a sleeping bag. If necessary, another warm person can be placed in the sleeping bag as well. As long as they can get to a warm place, hypothermia victims usually recover without emergency treatment.

The University of Alaska Anchorage Wilderness Studies Program includes such safety procedures in its classes on winter camping. Phone 907-786-4066.

Ski trails wind through the old buildings of Independence Mine at Hatcher Pass in the Talkeetna Mountains.

3. MATANUSKA-SUSITNA VALLEY

In the Matanuska-Susitna Valley, which stretches for miles along the Glenn and Parks highways between Anchorage and Fairbanks, are many mountains in the Chugach and Talkeetna Ranges that have excellent potential for both alpine and nordic skiing. Yet the population of the area has not been sufficient to support extensive development. Secondary road networks, which supported early twentieth-century gold-mining enterprises, allow access to some areas used by skiers, snowboarders, snow machiners, dog mushers, and even paragliders.

Hatcher Pass

Located eighteen miles north of Palmer and sixty miles from Anchorage in the Talkeetna Mountains, Hatcher Pass has lured both cross-country and downhill skiers since Independence Mine was in full operation in the 1930s. The mine area, at the head of a steep-walled valley with a base elevation of 3,580 feet, usually receives a consistent snow cover by the end of October — a full month before other Alaska ski areas — and retains skiable snow until late into the spring.

Interest in early skiing at Independence Mine can be traced back to Russell Dow, a former member of the Dartmouth ski team who came to Alaska with Bradford Washburn in the 1930s on the

Harvard-Dartmouth mapping expedition. While working as a tractor driver at Independence Mine, Dow began skiing down to Palmer to visit his girlfriend, Rusty, who ran the town laundry and later became one of the first truck drivers on the Alaska Highway. Other mine workers saw Dow skiing and decided it would be fun. Furthermore, since there were many single men at the mine and Palmer has the closest supply of single women, Dow soon had company on his trips to town.

Skiing soon became a popular recreational activity at the mine. Rows of skis lined the wall of the dormitory where the single miners lived and the territorial school attended by the children of married mine workers.

Residents in Palmer took up skiing as well. Claire Lewis Kopperud had no previous skiing experience when she came to work in the Palmer Hospital in 1937. In order to participate in this new sport enjoyed by the 375 "nice young men" at the mine, she purchased a pair of seven-foot wooden skis with cable bindings, and joined the ski expeditions between Independence Mine and Palmer. She attested to the skill of these early skiers, who pulled women down from the mine on sleds so they could deliver their babies at the Palmer Hospital.

When Independence Mine was forced to close during World War II, Dow took a job teaching soldiers to ski at Fort Richardson outside of Anchorage. He was also instrumental in forming the Anchorage Ski Club and building a rope tow at the Curry Hotel, an overnight stop on the Alaska Railroad north of Talkeetna.

After World War II, the price of gold was not high enough to justify reopening Independence Mine, so most of the buildings were left vacant, even though they had been built less than ten years before. Avid skiers still came up to the mine and camped in the buildings while they climbed and skied on the surrounding mountains. After the road to Palmer was completed, skiers from Anchorage

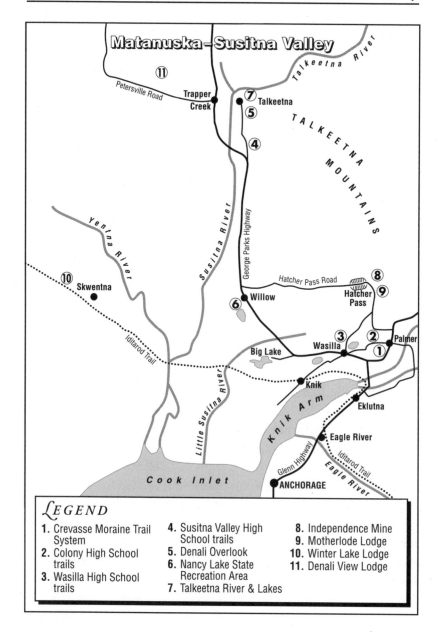

LEGEND

1. Crevasse Moraine Trail System
2. Colony High School trails
3. Wasilla High School trails
4. Susitna Valley High School trails
5. Denali Overlook
6. Nancy Lake State Recreation Area
7. Talkeetna River & Lakes
8. Independence Mine
9. Motherlode Lodge
10. Winter Lake Lodge
11. Denali View Lodge

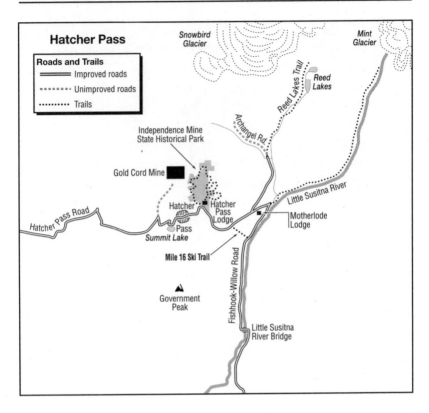

reached the Independence Mine area on weekends by taking a three-hour ride on a school bus.

For a while during the 1960s, rope tows and a T-bar were used at Independence Mine, and concessionaires housed and fed skiers in the newest bunkhouse. The United States Army Biathlon Team used the area for training during that decade because the snow cover was more reliable there than at Fort Richardson, which had been designated the Army Biathlon Training Center in 1958. Team members stayed in the bunkhouses and created their own rifle range. For targets, they stuck inflated balloons through holes in sheets of plywood. High school and college cross-country ski teams also used the area for early season training before the trails in town had enough snow.

By the 1970s, both alpine and nordic ski facilities had been developed closer to the population center in Anchorage, and the mine dormitories had so deteriorated that they were no longer suitable to house skiers. Private entrepreneurs, however, acquired the original Manager's House and refitted it as a bar and lodge for skiers and also for the snow machiners who were starting to discover the Hatcher Pass area.

Independence Mine acquired a new mission in the 1980s, when the price of gold increased sufficiently to tempt the owners to begin mining again. Deciding to approach the mine shafts from the other side of the mountain, they offered to donate the old mine buildings to the State of Alaska for a tax deduction. Independence Mine State Historical Park was created in 1980, and the state purchased the Manager's House for use as the visitor's center.

The state historical park is a popular summer tourist attraction, drawing up to 35,000 visitors annually, but is not open in the winter. The Hatcher Pass area, however, continues to attract a steady stream of winter sport enthusiasts. The Hatcher Pass Road to Willow is not open in the winter and is only plowed as far as the Hatcher Pass Lodge. A popular winter ski tour follows the unplowed Hatcher Pass Road across the pass toward Willow.

An A-frame building, the Hatcher Pass Lodge is one of two lodges in the area providing housing and full food service (phone 907-745-5897). The other, the Motherlode Lodge (phone 907-746-1464) is at Mile 14 of Fishhook-Willow Road, six miles below Independence Mine.

A private contractor grooms eighteen kilometers of cross-country ski trails for both skating and classical striding. For using these trails, skiers are charged a $5 daily fee, payable at the Hatcher Pass Lodge, where the trails begin. These picturesque trails wind among the old Independence Mine buildings and up to Gold Cord Mine in the next valley.

From the peak of the mountain (referred to as "4,068" for its elevation) descend the swirling, linked ski tracks made by alpine and telemark skiers. They are transported to the top by Glacier

SnowCat Skiing Tours, Inc., which advertises safe, affordable backcountry skiing and snowboarding on runs two to three miles long with descents of over 2,000 feet, of varying degrees of difficulty. The snowcat, which can accommodate twelve passengers, a ski-patroller, and the driver, boards at the Motherlode Lodge and gives clients access to as much as 20,000 vertical feet of untracked powder daily. For more information, write to: Glacier SnowCat Skiing Tours, Inc., P.O. Box 874234, Wasilla, AK 99687. Their hotline, 907-346-1276, provides snow condition reports in winter.

Glacier SnowCat Skiing Tours teaches its clients backcountry safety procedures and provides them with avalanche rescue beacons, but all other backcountry skiers, snowboarders, and snowmobilers are on their own. The Hatcher Pass area can be dangerous, and nearly every year some winter sports enthusiast is the victim of an avalanche or hypothermia.

Because of its relative accessibility and excellent terrain and snow conditions, the Hatcher Pass area continues to inspire dreams of further development. In 1988 the giant Japanese trading company Mitsui Corp. proposed to construct a $221 million resort complete with a golf course, a dude ranch, and an airport — only to pull out two years later when market studies failed to support the venture. Currently the Hatcher Pass Development Corp. has a state lease to develop a $23 million resort and ski area on 4,600-foot Government Peak, but no actual construction has taken place.

In the meantime, winter enthusiasts continue to use the area as they please. Local teenagers have developed their own Mile 16 run down to Fishhook-Willow Road, two miles below the Motherlode Lodge, where they hitch rides up the road as far as drivers will take them.

Crevasse Moraine Winter Trails

The Crevasse Moraine trail system, two miles from Palmer off the Palmer-Wasilla Highway at the end of Loma Prieta Drive, was developed and is maintained by the Matanuska-Susitna Borough Recreational Services Division. The trails traverse an area of moraine, where glaciers deposited accumulations of earth and stone. The resulting network of ridges and depressions presents the skier with challenging terrain.

A total of 10.8 kilometers of cross-country trail, wide enough for both skating and classical techniques, are arranged in a series of thirteen loops ranging from 0.6 to 2.2 kilometers. Winter users may be accompanied by their dogs, as long as they clean up after them and keep them under voice control. Additional information and trail conditions can be obtained by calling Matanuska-Susitna Borough Recreational Services at 907-745-9631.

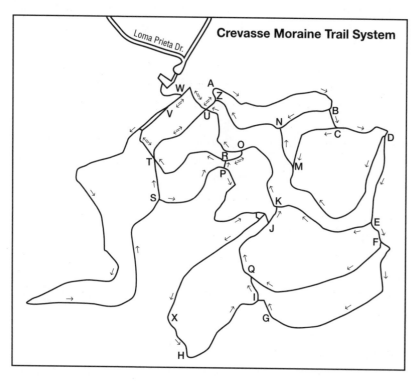

ELIZABETH TOWER

A grooming machine stands ready to start work on the Crevasse Moraine trail system near Palmer.

High School Trails

Adjacent to several high schools in the Matanuska-Susitna Valley are cross-country trails that are open to the public as well as to high school ski teams and students. Colony High School, at the intersection of 49th and Bogard Roads about four miles west of Palmer on the Palmer-Wasilla Highway, and Wasilla High School, at 701 E. Bogard Road, each maintain a 2.5-km trail. Susitna Valley High School also has a 2.5-km trail behind the school, which is located at Mile 98 on the Parks Highway at its intersection with the Talkeetna Spur Road.

These high school trails are not lighted for night skiing. If those not connected with the schools wish to use the trails, they should check in advance to make sure that they will not interfere with school teams in training.

Nancy Lake State Recreation Area

This 22,000-acre recreation area near Willow, encompassing 130 lakes and ponds between the Susitna River and the Talkeetna Mountains, is home to nearly ten miles of trail for skiing only, plus more than thirty miles of other multi-use trails. Visitors reach it by taking the Nancy Lake Parkway at Mile 67 of the Parks Highway. In the winter, the parkway is unplowed and closed beyond Mile 2.2, where there is a parking lot at the Winter Trailhead.

Located in the non-motorized area north of the parkway, the 9.7-mi. ski trail consists of three loop trails. The 3-mi. Parkway Trail, beginning and ending at the Winter Trailhead, offers good ski-touring through rolling, tree-covered hills. About 1.8 miles along the Parkway Trail, it connects with the Jano Pond Loop, which crosses 3.6 miles of frozen swamps and gentle hills. The third loop, covering 3.1 miles, is named for Rhein Lake, which it encircles.

Adventurous skiers can also try the recreation area's multi-use trails on the south side, which they may have to share with snowmachiners and dog mushers. The 15-mi. Red Shirt Lake Trail

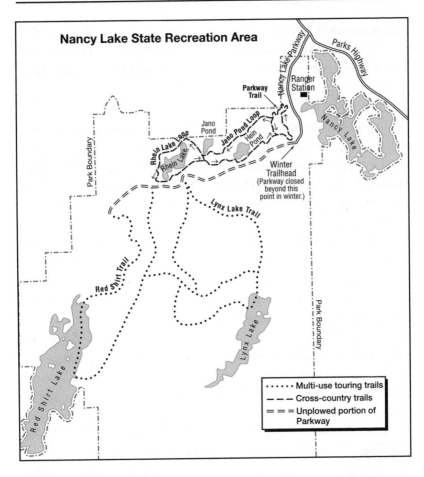

leads to the second largest body of water in the area, while the connected Lynx Lake Trail is a 13-mi. tour of thirteen lakes. The Nordic Skiing Association of Anchorage (phone 907-276-7609) schedules weekend tours to this area seventy miles north of Anchorage each year.

The park service rents twelve cabins in the recreation area, on Nancy Lake, Red Shirt Lake, Lynx Lake, and James Lake. Ask about them at the ranger station at Mile 1.3 of the parkway, or phone the Mat-Su Valley office of the Division of Parks and Outdoor

Recreation at 907-745-3975. Call the Nancy Lake office at 907-495-6273 for a pre-recorded message about weather conditions and recreation opportunities in the Nancy Lake State Recreation Area.

Denali and Talkeetna

The capable back-country skier who wants a unique and exciting wilderness skiing experience might consider spending several days on the slopes of North America's highest mountain. The Mountain House, situated at the 6,000-foot level of the Denali (McKinley) massif, was constructed on a five-acre rock and ice outcrop of the Ruth Glacier by legendary bush pilot Don Sheldon, as a modest shelter for mountaineers, skiers, photographers, and other wilderness-seekers. This circular, five-sided hut, approximately fourteen feet in diameter, is reached via a ten-minute trek up a snow slope from the glacier landing area. Glass windows offer breathtaking views, and four benches provide space for sleeping bags. A small, cast-iron woodstove in the center of the hut is used for heating but is not large enough for most cooking purposes. The Mountain House can accommodate five people comfortably; larger groups use the hut as a base of operations where skiers sleeping in tents can warm up and dry out.

Roberta Sheldon, widow of Don Sheldon, warns that the Mountain House is not for everyone. Although it is a rough, wooden hut on primitive terrain in an often unfriendly climate, most visitors appreciate it as a unique structure in a truly spectacular setting — to a wet or cold skier it can be a priceless haven from the elements. Even on warm summer days the mercurial Alaskan weather can alter conditions quickly, lowering temperatures and suddenly bringing wind and snow.

Crevasses are often present near the Mountain House property and skiers should always be aware of them, even though they have not caused problems in more than thirty years. This is glacial terrain, where it may be advisable to rope up. Those choosing to ski

79

here should have a reasonable amount of outdoor experience, and travel on the Ruth Glacier is not recommended for children. All visitors are required to sign an "Acknowledgment of Risk" and "Release of Liability" form in advance, verifying that they realize the inherent dangers of this wilderness experience.

The Mountain House is in use from March through mid-July, depending on seasonal conditions. Although in March days begin getting longer and temperatures become warmer, winter conditions still prevail; sudden storms can drop a lot of snow, causing visitors to be hut-bound and sometimes weathered in beyond their pick-up dates. May is usually considered the best month for both weather and snow. June is generally warm and beautiful, but the snow may be soft for skiing. Hot summer weather causes the glacier to deteriorate sometime around mid-July, and aircraft landing conditions may be marginal after that.

Visitors provide all their own gear, including sleeping bags, cooking utensils, stove, clothing, personal items, food, and wood. In 1997 the daily rental rate for the Mountain House was $85 for groups of five or less and $100 for larger groups. Bookings are on a first-come/first-served basis and should be made at least a year in advance. For more information about reservations and flying arrangements, contact Roberta Sheldon, Alaska Retreat, Box 292, Talkeetna, AK 99676. Phone 907-733-2414.

The University of Alaska Anchorage Wilderness Study Program offers two four-day credit courses on Ruth Glacier each year in March or April. The class on telemark and backcountry skiing, offered in conjunction with the North American Telemark Organization, uses the Mountain House, while students attending the mountaineering course are on their own. For more information on these classes, call the UAA Wilderness Study Program at 907-786-4066.

The staging point for mountain-climbing expeditions to Mt. McKinley and adjoining peaks is traditionally Talkeetna, an old

PATTY HAMRE

Several skiers, carefully roped up, approach the Moose's Tooth in Ruth Amphitheater on Mt. McKinley.

mining town 112 miles north of Anchorage on the Parks Highway. Several flight services in town fly skiers to Ruth Glacier, which has become a favorite springtime area for touring and telemarking. In addition to transporting skiers, climbers, campers, and sightseers to the mountain, K2 Aviation also maintains a climbers' bunkhouse in Talkeetna that can provide inexpensive accommodation for up to eighteen people. Contact K2 Aviation at Box 545-B, Talkeetna, AK 99676, or phone 907-733-2291 or fax 907-733-1221.

Roberta Sheldon recommends Doug Geeting Aviation, Box 42, Talkeetna, AK 99676, phone 907-733-2366. Other air taxi operations that provide glacier landings include Talkeetna Air Taxi Inc., phone 907-733-2219 or 800-533-2219, and Hudson Air Service, 907-733-2321.

While awaiting a flight to Denali or using the area's trail systems, skiers can stay in one of Talkeetna's historic bed-and-breakfasts.

Dating back to the early 1900s, Belle's Cabin (operated by Roberta Sheldon) is a lovely log cabin originally owned by Belle Lee McDonald, a hard-working trading post operator who lived in Talkeetna for forty years. Write to Alaska Retreat, Box 292, Talkeetna, AK 99676. Phone 907-733-2414. Other lodgings in historic local buildings include the Talkeetna Roadhouse on Talkeetna's Main Street (phone 907-733-1351), and Trapper John's Bed-and-Breakfast, which advertises a "full sourdough breakfast" and a "5-star outhouse" (P.O. Box 243, Talkeetna, AK 99676).

The Talkeetna area offers a number of trails that can be used for cross-country touring. In past years these trails were regularly groomed, and the town frequently hosted cross-country races. The trails are now being used by an increasing number of dog mushers, however, and are no longer as smooth and aesthetically pleasing as dedicated cross-country skiers would like them to be.

Local skiing enthusiasts are forming their own nordic ski club and developing a 2.5-km loop trail. Starting at what's called the Denali Overlook — a parking lot along the road into Talkeetna with a gorgeous view of the McKinley Range — this new trail promises to be one of the most scenic trails in Alaska. The new ski club also is planning touring trails through the Talkeetna Lakes. For more information and an up-to-date map, contact the Denali Nordic Ski Club, Box 754, Talkeetna, AK 99676.

Another interesting Talkeetna option is offered by Mountain Hound Mush!, which advertises dog-supported backcountry ski trips with expedition equipment and food freighting — and gourmet cocoa. Write to Box 339, Talkeetna, AK 99676 or phone 907-733-1351.

SPOTLIGHT: Iditasport

The annual March sled dog race to Nome isn't the only race run on the historic Iditarod Trail. For several years, cross-country skiers ran the 170-mi. Iditaski Race from Big Lake to Skwentna and back a week before the sled dog race began. In 1991 the Iditaski

Race merged with the Iditabike Race to form what is now known as the Iditasport. The race allows an interesting opportunity to compare the speeds of skiers with those of mountain bikers. Runners and snowshoers compete in a shorter 85-mi. course.

The conventional wisdom is that biking is generally the fastest way to finish the Iditasport. Light snowfall in 1996 gave bikers excellent training conditions and made the course look particularly rideable. But then a heavy snowstorm shortly before the race gave the leading skier, Jim Jager of Anchorage, an advantage early in the race. Once the trail set up and got faster after sunset, John Samstead of Cincinnati passed Jager on a bike. Jager held on to take second place overall, finishing the race in 25 hours and 25 minutes, less than two hours slower than the winner and two hours ahead of the next biker. Two female skiers and one female biker finished the race, the biker beating the leading skier by seven hours.

The Skarland Trail System starts at the ski hut on the west ridge of the University of Alaska Fairbanks.

4. FAIRBANKS AREA

Skiing is a popular form of recreation in Interior Alaska through-out the winter even though the average maximum temperature during the month of January is below zero and temperatures occasionally drop to 50 below. Three alpine ski areas in or near Fairbanks — Birch Hill, Skiland, and Moose Mountain — are open from November through April when the temperature is above 20 degrees below zero. From mid-February until the close of the season, temperatures can vary considerably throughout the day. On a bright, sunny March morning with the thermometer registering 20 below in Fairbanks, the ski report may truthfully invite skiers to enjoy another lovely day of downhill skiing.

Continued physical activity allows cross-country skiers to tolerate lower temperatures than alpine skiers. Early snow in October and November, before the coldest months, often make trails in the Fairbanks area available for recreational and competitive skiing before sufficient snow cover has occurred elsewhere in Alaska. By mid-February and early March, when days are getting longer, bright sunshine raises temperatures to 20 or 30 degrees above zero during the day, even though night temperatures frequently fall below zero. A number of cross-country trail systems with varying degrees of sophistication and difficulty have been developed in the Fairbanks area since the 1930s.

The Golden Age of Skiing at UAF

The University of Alaska Fairbanks, which opened in September 1922 as the Alaska Agricultural College and School of Mines, played a pivotal part in the development of skiing in the Fairbanks area. Ski races were held there as early as 1924, but the major boost to skiing came with the arrival of Ivar Skarland, a native Norwegian, in 1931. Skarland, an excellent skier, instructed fellow students in technique. With Inge Trigstad, he developed the first racing trail on campus and constructed a ski jump on "Engineer Hill."

The growth of skiing in Alaska during the 1930s was hampered by the difficulty of acquiring skis. When Skarland ordered seven pairs of skis and poles from Norway in the summer of 1933, the order took five months by boat via the Panama Canal and didn't arrive until January 1934. Some skiers were forced to design and construct their own skis from local timber. Although Norwegians used hickory for durability in rugged country, Alaskan white birch, if properly seasoned, was also an excellent material for skis.

As Skarland helped other students procure skis from Scandinavia, skiing became an integral part of college life. An experienced skier could cover the well-used ski route to town and back in thirty-five to forty minutes, and a 4-mi. trail on campus was in continual use. Many students were able to ski between college and their weekend jobs in nearby mines. Money from these jobs enabled them to buy the finest ski equipment available from Sweden.

A college ski club was formed during the winter of 1935-6, and University President Charles Bunnell donated a cabin on property he owned about three miles from the campus. On November 14, 1936, about forty skiers dedicated the cabin, which became the center of recreational activity. For many years Dr. Bunnell hosted an annual fried chicken feed at the cabin. In the surrounding area the student skiers cut trails, built a jump, and set up a slalom course. The trails were only wide enough to maneuver through the trees,

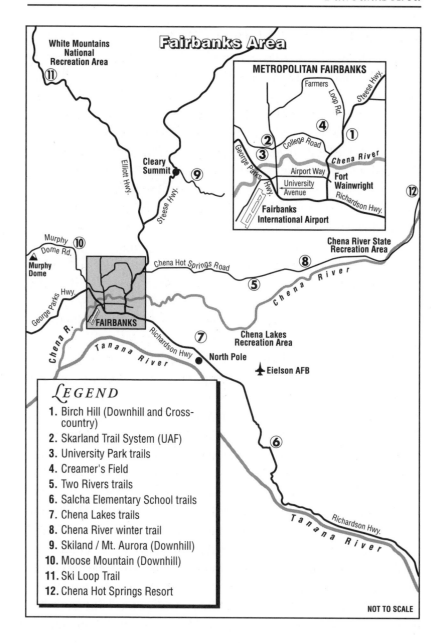

Fairbanks Area

White Mountains
National
Recreation Area

⑪

METROPOLITAN FAIRBANKS

Farmers

Loop Rd.

Steese Hwy.

④ ①

College Road

② ③

Chena River

George Parks Hwy.

Airport Way

University Avenue

Fort Wainwright

Richardson Hwy.

⑫

Fairbanks
International Airport

Elliott Hwy.

Cleary Summit ⑨

Steese Hwy.

Murphy Dome Rd. ⑩

Murphy Dome

Chena Hot Springs Road

Chena River State Recreation Area

⑧

⑤ Chena River

George Parks Hwy.

Chena R.

FAIRBANKS

Richardson Hwy.

Tanana River

⑦ Chena Lakes Recreation Area

North Pole

Eielson AFB

⑥

Tanana River

Richardson Hwy.

LEGEND

1. Birch Hill (Downhill and Cross-country)
2. Skarland Trail System (UAF)
3. University Park trails
4. Creamer's Field
5. Two Rivers trails
6. Salcha Elementary School trails
7. Chena Lakes trails
8. Chena River winter trail
9. Skiland / Mt. Aurora (Downhill)
10. Moose Mountain (Downhill)
11. Ski Loop Trail
12. Chena Hot Springs Resort

NOT TO SCALE

and everyone who used the trails contributed to their construction and maintenance, carrying axes with them to brush and straighten trails as needed. Skiers were so familiar with them that no trail maps were ever needed.

Ivar Skarland graduated in the spring of 1935, just before the Alaska legislature renamed the college the University of Alaska. After graduate study at Harvard University, he returned to the University of Alaska as a professor of anthropology, a position he held for two decades. As a cross-country skier, Skarland was in a class by himself. He helped conduct the 1939 U.S. Census by skiing along the Alaska Railroad in mid-winter.

Skiing was recognized as a varsity sport in 1941, but World War II brought drastic changes at the university. Enrollment declined and athletic programs were dropped between 1943 and 1948. Even though the ski club lingered on with smaller numbers, it could not sustain the popularity it enjoyed in its formative years. The "golden age" was over, but that era and Skarland's influence are recalled by the Skarland Trail System near the university.

Skarland Ski Trail System

A number of outdoor enthusiasts, including veterans of the 10th Mountain Division who came to Fairbanks in the post-War period to work or go to school, regularly commuted to and from the University of Alaska on skis. When land adjoining the university was subdivided, activists like Celia Hunter and Ginny Wood, who had ferried planes to Alaska on the Lend-Lease program and later settled in the area, were instrumental in seeing that non-motorized trail easements were included in the subdivision plats.

During the mid-1950s the university ski team cleared a 9-mi. trail, which they connected to the subdivision trails so that a 12-mi. circuit originated on campus and wound through the neighboring wooded hillsides. Jim Mahaffey, an Olympic skier who had trained under Sven Wik in Colorado, took over the

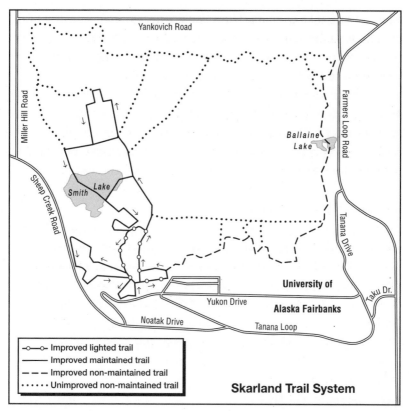

Skarland Trail System

Legend:
- ○—○ Improved lighted trail
- —— Improved maintained trail
- – – – Improved non-maintained trail
- ····· Unimproved non-maintained trail

university coaching job in 1962 and enhanced the trails to vary in difficulty.

After Dr. Ivar Skarland's death in 1965, the state approved the student body's recommendation to formally name the 12-mi. trail the Skarland Ski Trail System. In 1980 the North Star Borough and the university entered into a Memorandum of Understanding, which provides that the university will include preservation of the trail in future campus planning and development. The Skarland Ski Trail System was formally dedicated in September 1982.

Currently the Skarland Ski Trail System offers twenty kilometers of recreational trail that is cleared but not groomed. The trails begin and end at the ski hut on the west ridge of the University of

Alaska Fairbanks campus. They also are accessible at several other points along Ballaine Road and at the Musk Ox Farm. The west ridge ski hut also provides access to five kilometers of well-groomed trails with one kilometer lighted from dark until 10 p.m.

Probably the best source of current information about the condition of this and other cross-country trail systems in Fairbanks is a sporting goods store called Beaver Sports (see sidebar), phone 907-479-2494. Also, the *Fairbanks Daily News-Miner* carries up-to-date information on the status of local ski trails.

University Park Trails

Cross-country skiing has become such an integral part of school athletic programs that several schools in the Fairbanks area have developed their own trails. University Park Elementary School (554 Loftus Road) and West Valley High School (3800 Geist Road) in west Fairbanks share 1-km and 2.5-km loops that are accessible from both school parking lots. Open to the public, these trails are not always groomed and are not lighted. For trail conditions, call Beaver Sports at 907-479-2494.

Two Rivers Trails

A more extensive trail system has been developed behind Two Rivers Elementary School, eighteen miles from Fairbanks. It's reached by taking Chena Hot Springs Road to Mile 18.5, then following a sign to Two Rivers Elementary School, which is set back about a half-mile from Chena Hot Springs Road. This trail system consists of a 1-km lighted loop in addition to 2.5-km, 5-km, and 7.5-km trails of varying difficulty, with some steep downhills on the outer loops. The trails are open at all times and are usually groomed, but the lights have to be turned on by skiers. For trail conditions, call Beaver Sports at 907-479-2494.

A FAMILY BUSINESS
Beaver Sports

The Whisenhant family in Fairbanks became involved in the sporting goods business out of a background in nordic skiing. Jim Whisenhant, a former University of Alaska skier, taught at Lathrop High School and coached the cross-country ski team from 1960 until 1978. As a hobby he began selling cross-country ski gear, canoes, and other sports equipment that was difficult to acquire in Fairbanks during the early 1970s. Initially he stored his inventory in his garage and only opened after school hours.

When he acquired two small buildings on College Road, Whisenhant added bicycles, camping gear, and a large selection of other recreational equipment. Beaver Sports now carries almost all kinds of sporting goods except for guns and motorized vehicles.

The current store at 3480 College Road opened in 1987.

During the Alyeska pipeline boom in the late 1970s, the Whisenhants recognized the need for a sporting goods store in Valdez. They started a branch of Beaver Sports there, now managed by Whisenhant's son Chris. Jim Whisenhant, who has retired from teaching and coaching, continues to serve as general manager of the Fairbanks store. His son Greg, a former cross-country competitor who grew up with the business, now serves as an assistant manager of Beaver Sports in Fairbanks, and a Whisenhant daughter, Elise Miller, is the advertising manager. A good source of reliable information about ski equipment and the condition of local ski trails, Beaver Sports can be reached at 907-479-2494.

Salcha Trails

A challenging 15-km trail system is located next to Salcha Elementary School, thirty-seven miles southeast of Fairbanks on the Richardson Highway. These trails are groomed for both skating and striding, and are frequently used for statewide school races. The 2.5 kilometers adjacent to the school are lighted when students are practicing. The Salcha Nordic Ski Club, which maintains the trails, can be reached at 907-488-3987.

Chena Lakes Recreation Area

Cross-country skiers dreaming of an easy, quiet tour through birch forest on flat, narrow trails groomed for diagonal striding should try the 6.5 kilometers of trail in the Chena Lakes Recreational Area. To reach these trails, turn off the Richardson Highway fourteen miles from Fairbanks, following signs to the park entrance, and continue 2.5 miles into the park. The trails, which start at a picnic shelter, are used as nature trails in the summer. For more information, contact the Fairbanks North Star Borough Parks and Recreation Department, P.O. Box 71267, Fairbanks, AK 99707; phone 907-459-1070.

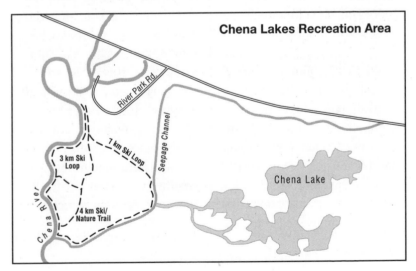

ELIZABETH TOWER

In the Chena Lakes Recreation Area, flat, narrow trails lead cross-country skiers through birch forests.

Chena River State Recreation Area

Twenty-six miles east of Fairbanks on Chena Hot Springs Road, the Chena River State Recreation Area covers 250,000 acres of hills and valleys along the crystal-clear Chena River. A popular trail system is extensively used by skiers, snowshoers, and snowmachiners whenever snow is on the ground, regardless of the temperature.

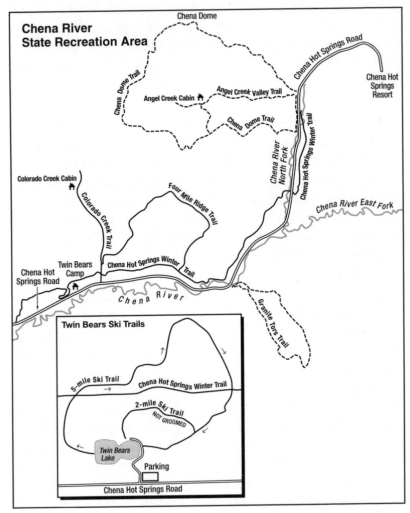

Well-marked with color-coded signs, the trails are regularly groomed but not tracked for diagonal skiing.

The 6.2-mi. Nugget Creek Trail, the 5.8-mi. Colorado Creek Trail, and the Angel Creek Trail are multi-use trails, also used by dog mushers and snowmachiners. However, the Granite Tors Trail, a 15-mi. loop, is for non-mechanized use only. Cabins at the end of the trails are good places to warm up afterward. Also, the 3-mi. and 2-mi. trails at Twin Bears Camp are for cross-country skiers only, and are occasionally groomed. For more information, contact the Alaska State Parks, Northern Region Office, 3700 Airport Way, Fairbanks, AK 99709, or call 907-451-2695.

White Mountains National Recreation Area

This one-million-acre recreation area, twenty-eight miles northwest of Fairbanks along the Elliott Highway, offers a network of 200 miles of winter trails through a variety of terrain, from rolling hills to steep mountain passes. Skiers will find the trailhead with signs and information boards along the Elliott Highway; trail routes are along corridors in wooded areas and marked with tripods and reflective trail markers in open areas.

All trails are open to motorized vehicles and are therefore used by snowmachiners — except for the Ski Loop Trail, a moderately challenging 5-mi. trail that starts at the White Mountains Trailhead on the Elliott Highway. This loop trail follows the Summit Trail up to an overlook of Mt. McKinley and the Alaska Range, then heads back to the trailhead via the Wickersham Creek Trail.

Ten public-use cabins are located along various trails throughout the recreation area, available for $20 per night in 1997. For more information on the trails or the cabins, or to make reservations, contact the Bureau of Land Management (BLM) Land Information Office, 1150 University Avenue, Fairbanks, AK 99709-2250 (phone 907-474-2251).

The BLM also maintains a website with detailed information

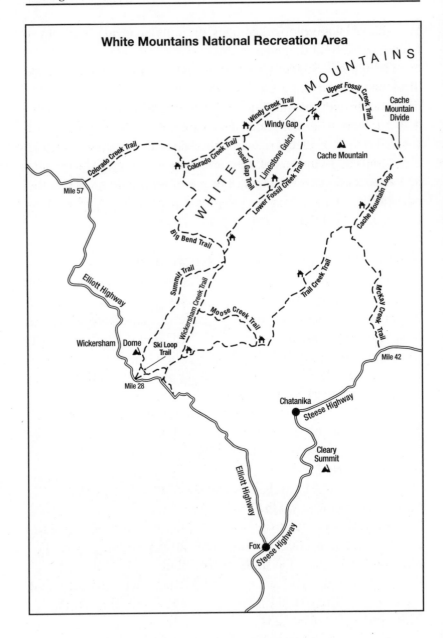

White Mountains National Recreation Area

and photos of the maps and trails: http://www.aurora.ak.blm.gov/ WhiteMtns.

Birch Hill Recreation Area

Tremendous growth in the popularity of cross-country skiing in Fairbanks during the late 1960s and 1970s, combined with the development of plastic skis and the skating technique, placed new demands on the already crowded university trails. In 1968, Jim Whisenhant, one of the early post-War university skiers who was coaching the Lathrop High School ski team, discovered a 200-acre plot of land on the northwestern slope of Birch Hill that the State of Alaska was leasing to the city of Fairbanks for a dollar a year. Since there was only one year remaining on the lease and the city had no plans for the area, Whisenhant received permission to have his ski

Cross-Country Etiquette

At the Birch Hill Ski Trails on the east side of Fairbanks, the Nordic Ski Club of Fairbanks and Fairbanks North Star Borough have posted this sign, giving cross-country skiers a useful lesson in trail safety and courtesy:

❋ During the winter, specified nordic ski trails are to be used for nordic skiing only. No sleds, snowshoes, or motorized vehicles are permitted.

❋ Ski only trail loops within your ski level.

❋ When approaching a slower skier in your lane with intent to pass, shout "Track" well in advance.

❋ When a skier shouts "Track" with intent to pass, step off the trail immediately, giving the skier plenty of room as well as the right of way.

❋ Be particularly aware of other skiers when skiing the trails in tandem.

❋ Do not stop on trails.

ELIZABETH TOWER

Snowboarders look down on Fort Wainwright from the top of Birch Hill, to the east of downtown Fairbanks.

team cut and maintain ski trails that would meet the requirements necessary for the city or borough to renew the lease.

By 1977, the Birch Hill trails were sufficiently developed to host the United States Junior National Ski Races and the Alaska High School State Championship. International races, drawing teams from across the United States, Sweden, Switzerland, Norway, Finland, Canada, West Germany, and Australia were held at Birch Hill in 1984.

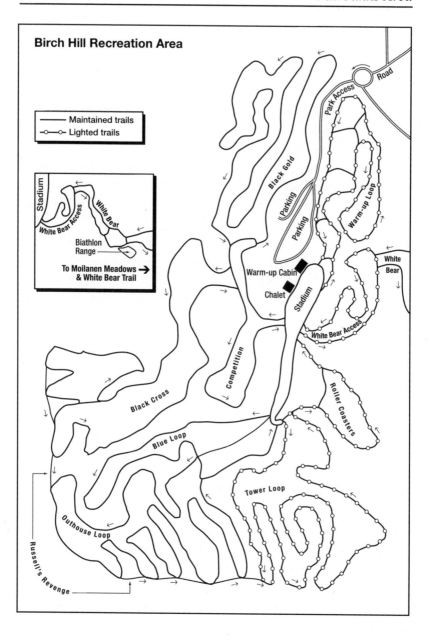

Birch Hill Recreation Area

Maintained trails
Lighted trails

Stadium
White Bear Access
White Bear
Biathlon Range
To Moilanen Meadows & White Bear Trail

Black Gold
Park Access Road
Parking
Parking
Warm-up Loop
White Bear
Warm-up Cabin
Chalet
Stadium
White Bear Access
Competition
Roller Coasters
Black Cross
Blue Loop
Tower Loop
Outhouse Loop
Russell's Revenge

Today the Birch Hill Recreation Area offers twenty-six kilometers of trail, groomed for both diagonal striding and skating. The trails vary in difficulty, and approximately six kilometers are lighted until 9:30 p.m. The trails are reached by turning right off the Steese Highway opposite Farmers Loop Road and following Birch Hill Road for two miles to the Birch Hill Recreation Area; signs point the way.

The trail system is maintained by the Nordic Ski Club of Fairbanks in cooperation with the Fairbanks North Star Borough. For more information, contact the Fairbanks North Star Borough Parks and Recreation Department, P.O. Box 71267, Fairbanks, AK 99707; phone 907-459-1070. Or write to the Nordic Ski Club of Fairbanks, P.O. Box 80111, Fairbanks, AK 99708.

Birch Hill Alpine Ski Area

Although just on the other side of the Birch Hill Recreation Area, this downhill skiing area is on military property, overlooking Fort Wainwright and operated by Fort Wainwright Outdoor Recreation. The slopes are open to the general public Thursday through Sunday, with lights for evening skiing. Birch Hill's broad, open slopes are served by a double chairlift, which was installed several years ago. There's also an attractive base lodge and a complete rental shop for both skiers and snowboarders. After entering Fort Wainwright through the main gate in downtown Fairbanks, follow signs to the ski area. For a report on skiing conditions, call the Snow Phone Info Line at 907-353-7053.

Skiland / Mt. Aurora

Skiland, on Cleary Summit east of the Steese Highway at Mile 20.5, started operation in 1962 with two rope tows. (An adjoining ski area which opened in 1959 is now closed.) The Skiland rope tows were replaced in February 1992 by "The Silver Express," a 3,800-foot double chairlift. A total of twenty-eight trails, varying in difficulty, descend 1,057 vertical feet from the lodge at the top of

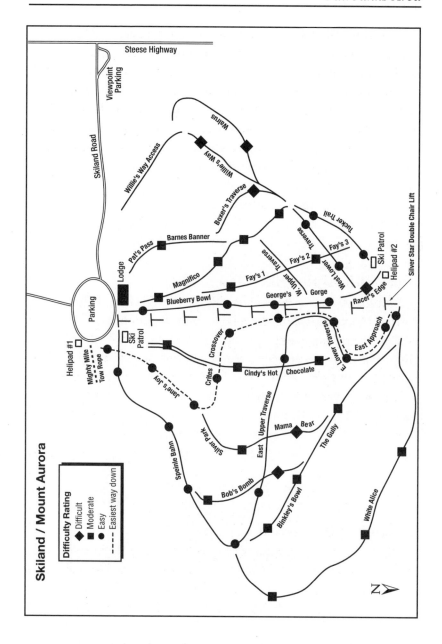

Skiland / Mount Aurora

Difficulty Rating
◆ Difficult
■ Moderate
● Easy
---- Easiest way down

the hill; some skiing is also possible between the trees. Ski instruction, food, and rental equipment are all available at Skiland.

During periods when Fairbanks experiences extremely cold temperature, Skiland is frequently enjoying a temperature inversion due to its higher elevation. Since Skiland's slopes have a northern exposure, skiing lasts well into the spring. Current ski conditions are reported at 907-459-ISKI or 907-459-4754, and the office phone is 907-389-2314. Or for more information write to Box 75310, Fairbanks, AK 99707.

ELIZABETH TOWER

A ski bus waits to transport skiers up Moose Mountain.

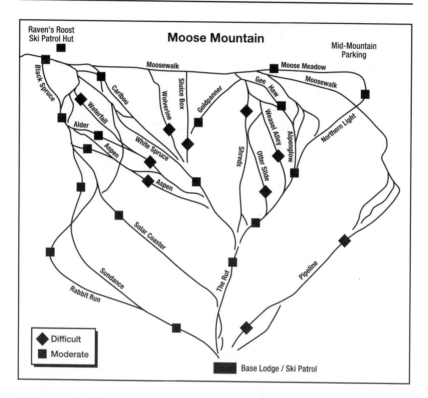

Moose Mountain

Twenty minutes from Fairbanks off Murphy Dome Road near its intersection with Spinach Creek Road, Moose Mountain has been open for four years. Rather than employing a chairlift, Moose Mountain uses a fleet of ski buses to transport skiers to the top of the mountain in welcome comfort and warmth. Usually ten buses are in use each day Thursday through Sunday when the temperature is above -20 degrees Fahrenheit and daily in March. Depending on the arrival of sufficient snow, Moose Mountain might open anytime from late October to mid-November and stay open until the snow melts in April. Each of its buses, which can carry thirty skiers, makes about ten runs a day from 10 a.m. until 5 p.m. or dusk.

The twenty-six runs on Moose Mountain, which are broad and

well-groomed, are separated by some forested areas that can be skied. Because Moose Mountain faces south, it is relatively warm during the cold season but does not keep snow late into the spring.

Ski instruction, food, and ski and snowshoe rentals are available. For more information, call the Moose Mountain office at 907-479-8362 or write to Box 84198, Fairbanks, AK 99708. For weather conditions, call 907-459-8132.

WARNING: Frostbite

Frostbite is usually not a serious consideration for skiers in Southeast and Southcentral Alaska, where daytime temperatures are rarely below zero. In Fairbanks and other Interior places, however, temperatures frequently fall far below zero. When the thermometer registers less than -20 degrees Fahrenheit during the day, alpine ski areas close down and cross-country races are cancelled. Cross-country tours use -15 as a cut-off. Even dedicated Fairbanks skiers would rather run than ski when it is colder than -20, because the cold snow is so slow that skiing is no longer enjoyable.

Experienced Fairbanks skiers have these suggestions for enjoyment and safety when exercising in the cold. Classical skiing is easier than skating. Some ski racers like Neoprene face masks, but others prefer neck gaiters and balaclavas because they help maintain moisture in the air passages of the body, especially the trachea and bronchi, against the onslaught of cold, dry air. Drinking lots of water also helps make up for the loss of moisture from lung tissues. Fairbanksans make a special effort to drink extra fluids before skiing, rather than carrying extra water that may freeze. After skiing, some people may experience coughing spasms when their lungs try to generate moisture with mucus. At extremely cold temperatures some ski glasses, designed to be aerodynamic, may freeze to the face. Eyeglasses fogging up can also be a problem, and soft contact lenses are usually more satisfactory.

Faces, feet, and fingers are most susceptible to frostbite. Mittens, rather than gloves, and overboots help protect the fingers and toes. Noses and earlobes that are in danger of frostbite will start to turn white, so the most important tip for skiing in cold weather is to go with a buddy or group who will keep an eye out for these early signs of frostbite. Judicious rewarming is the treatment of choice for mild frostbite unless continued exposure is unavoidable. Alternate freezing and thawing should be avoided.

Roughly sixty miles from Anchorage on the Seward Highway, Turnagain Pass is a favorite telemarking and ski touring area.

5. KENAI PENINSULA

Road-accessible mountains in the Chugach National Forest on the Kenai Peninsula south of Anchorage have long been a favorite playground of Alaska skiers. Small, portable rope tows no longer dot the slopes as they did in the days before Alyeska Resort opened at Girdwood in the 1960s, but cross-country skiers still enjoy touring on the east side of the Seward Highway at Turnagain Pass, and telemark skiers and snowboarders still climb the slopes of Tincan Mountain. Snowfall is heavy in these mountains, coming earlier in the fall and lasting longer than in other places, assuring good spring touring. However, avalanches are an ever-present danger and can rule out use of some Forest Service trails that pass through narrow canyons.

Skiers heading west on the Kenai Peninsula, along the Sterling Highway, will find several cross-country trail systems in the vicinity of Kenai and Soldotna, along Cook Inlet. More cross-country opportunities await on the southern peninsula around Homer, where scenic trails overlook lovely Katchemak Bay.

For skiers living or staying in Anchorage, reaching some of these ski areas will require a bit of a drive — from Anchorage it's 127 miles to Seward, 150 miles to Soldotna, or 230 miles to Homer. Those seeking something closer to the city might consider boarding the ski train for weekend skiing at Grandview.

The Great Alaska Ski Train

Before World War II, when there were no roads leading out of the Anchorage area, skiers had to rely on the Alaska Railroad for trips into the backcountry. Trains took skiers on weekend excursions to Wasilla, where they boarded buses to take them to Independence Mine at Hatcher Pass, or to the Curry Hotel north of Talkeetna, where they could use a rope tow. In 1941, the Alaska Railroad ran the first ski train to Grandview, midway between Anchorage and Seward, so passengers could ski on slopes near the tracks or tour back to Trail and Bartlett Glaciers.

Times changed after the war. The Curry Hotel burned down, and new rope tows pulled skiers to challenging slopes at Arctic

ANCHORAGE MUSEUM OF HISTORY AND ART

Passengers load their skis for a trip on board the Grandview Ski Train in 1944.

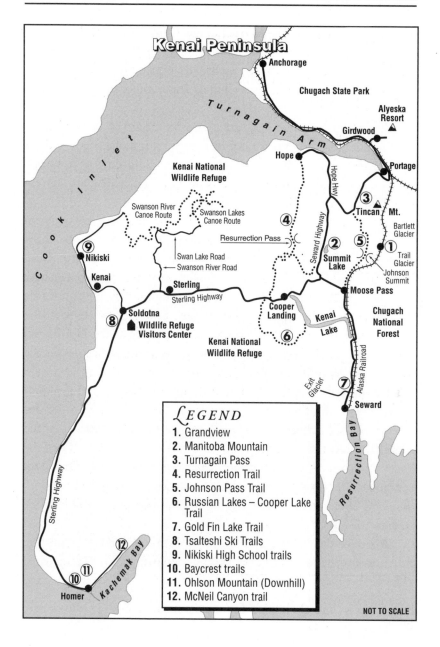

Kenai Peninsula

Anchorage

Chugach State Park

Alyeska Resort

Girdwood

Portage

Hope

Kenai National Wildlife Refuge

Tincan   Mt.

Bartlett Glacier

Swanson River Canoe Route

Swanson Lakes Canoe Route

4

3

5

1

Trail Glacier

Johnson Summit

Resurrection Pass

9
Nikiski

2
Summit Lake

Kenai

Swan Lake Road

Swanson River Road

Sterling

Sterling Highway

Cooper Landing

Moose Pass

Chugach National Forest

8
Soldotna
Wildlife Refuge Visitors Center

6

Kenai Lake

Kenai National Wildlife Refuge

Exit Glacier

7

Alaska Railroad

Seward

*L*EGEND
1. Grandview
2. Manitoba Mountain
3. Turnagain Pass
4. Resurrection Trail
5. Johnson Pass Trail
6. Russian Lakes – Cooper Lake Trail
7. Gold Fin Lake Trail
8. Tsalteshi Ski Trails
9. Nikiski High School trails
10. Baycrest trails
11. Ohlson Mountain (Downhill)
12. McNeil Canyon trail

12

Sterling Highway

Resurrection Bay

11

10
Homer

Kachemak Bay

Cook Inlet

Turnagain Arm

Hope Hwy

Seward Highway

NOT TO SCALE

109

Valley, conveniently close to Anchorage. Construction of the Seward Highway in the early 1950s made ski slopes on the Kenai Peninsula accessible by car, so the Alaska Railroad stopped running Grandview ski trains until the Nordic Ski Club of Anchorage resurrected them in the early 1970s.

Since then, trips on "the great Alaska ski train" have become much-anticipated events for nordic skiers, taking place two or three times a year, in February or March, on select Saturdays or Sundays. Souvenir ski train T-shirts, specially designed each year, are so treasured that they have become collector's items.

Ski trains leave Anchorage at 7:30 in the morning and arrive at Grandview around 10 a.m., after a brief stop in Portage to allow additional skiers to board. Much of the fun is in the train trip itself. A regular highlight is the live music provided by the German "Anchorage Krausenspieler" Band. Throughout the morning ride the band moves through the train, playing a song or two in each car. Also wandering through the trains are members of the Nordic Ski Patrol and the Forest Service, who provide information on the weather, ski conditions, and safety precautions.

Upon their arrival at Grandview, approximately 650 skiers of all ages and abilities clamp on their skis and disperse in various directions. Some head south on a 6-mi. tour to Trail Glacier, while others turn north to a ridge overlooking Bartlett Glacier. When the snow conditions are favorable, telemarkers can find excellent untracked snow along the east and west ridges after climbing with skins for about an hour. The Nordic Ski Patrol stays on duty all day to care for minor injuries.

After the trains turn around, they return to Grandview to serve as warm-up shelters until their prompt departure at 4:30 p.m. Most skiers bring picnic lunches with them to eat at Grandview, but some take advantage of the snack bars and beer bars on board the train cars.

Once the ski trains have departed from Grandview, and the band

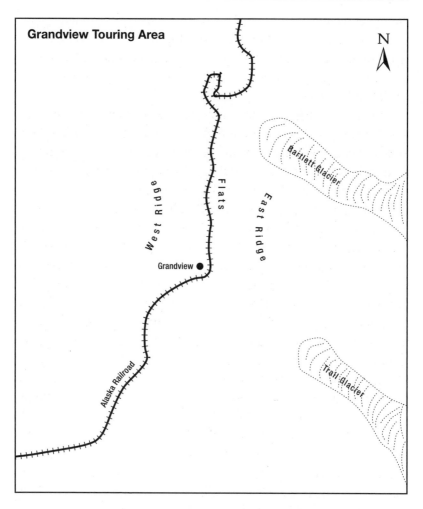

Grandview Touring Area

members' lips have recovered from a day of skiing, the Anchorage Krausenspieler Band gets back to work, providing music for the polka party in an appropriately decorated baggage car. Polka dancing continues all the way back to Anchorage, with the train swaying to the beat.

Ski train trips are usually scheduled for two spring weekends between the Anchorage Fur Rendevous and the Tour of Anchorage ski race. For more information, contact the Nordic Skiing Association of Anchorage, P.O. Box 10-3504, Anchorage, AK 99510-3504. Phone 907-276-7609 during the ski season.

ELIZABETH TOWER

Near Soldotna, touring trails surround the visitors center for the Kenai National Wildlife Refuge.

Along the Seward Highway

After winding around the east end of Turnagain Arm and parting ways with the tracks of the Alaska Railroad, the Seward Highway leads through Turnagain Pass, a favorite wintertime recreation area for snowmachiners and nordic skiers alike. The cross-country skiers and telemarkers tend to favor the east side of the highway because it is closed to motorized vehicles, but some do venture onto the hills along the west side. Some caution is necessary — extreme snow depths on the west side (up to twelve feet) mean that avalanches are common.

About five miles farther south on the Seward Highway is the north trailhead for the Johnson Pass trail. Although there is good skiing for about the first two miles of the trail, after that the area is hazardous because of serious avalanche danger. Skiing is also fairly safe on the first three miles from the other end of the trail, at Mile 32 of the Seward Highway. The entire 23-mi. traverse, passing Bench Lake and Johnson Lake, follows some of the original Iditarod Trail to Seward.

The 38-mi. Resurrection Pass Trail, from Hope to Cooper Landing, is a popular route for touring groups in the spring when days are getting longer. The trail follows Resurrection Creek for eighteen miles up to Resurrection Pass, elevation 2,600 feet, then slopes down to the Sterling Highway, paralleling Juneau Creek. Strong skiers can make the tour in one day under ideal conditions, but a series of nine Forest Service cabins along the trail can be rented by groups wishing to make the trip in a more leisurely fashion. The Forest Service does not groom the trail in winter, but frequent use by snowmachines usually results in packed tracks to follow. For more information on the trail or the cabins, contact the Alaska Public Lands Information Center, 605 West Fourth Avenue, Suite 105, Anchorage, AK 99501. Phone 907-271-2737.

Manitoba Mountain, near Summit Lake, is another popular destination for telemark skiers. A cabin at the base of the mountain, maintained by the Nordic Skiing Association of Anchorage, is available for use by its members. Summit Lake Lodge (phone 907-595-1520), at Mile 45 of the Seward Highway, has cabins and an attractive restaurant.

Several bed-and-breakfasts at Moose Pass stay open in the winter and welcome skiers: Alpenglow Cottage (phone 907-288-3142), the Spruce Moss B and B (phone 907-288-3667), and Crown Point Lodge (phone 907-288-3136).

About eleven miles north of Seward are some practice trails around Gold Fin Lake, groomed by the Seward High School cross-country ski team. Seven miles farther south, a 9-mi. ski trail maintained by the Forest Service leads to Exit Glacier. During the summer this is one of the most accessible glaciers in Alaska, but the road to the glacier is closed in the winter. Trails starting at the ranger station lead to the base of the glacier and to the Harding Icefield.

Along the Sterling Highway to Kenai / Soldotna

At Mile 37.7 of the Seward Highway, northwest of Moose Pass, it connects with the Sterling Highway, which leads about sixty miles west to Kenai, Soldotna, and Nikiski. By turning onto Snug Harbor Road at Mile 48 of the highway, then following the road along the lake for eight miles, skiers can reach the start of the Forest Service trail through the hills around Cooper Lake. Beginning at the fork in Snug Harbor Road, the trail leads twenty-three miles to the Russian River Campground back on the Sterling Highway. Skiers will find good telemarking between North Peak and Endo Peak, then can continue past Upper Russian Lake, along the Russian River, and onto Lower Russian Lake. However, caution is necessary around Lower Russian Lake, where avalanches often occur after storms.

Farther west on the Sterling Highway, travelers cross into the 2-million-acre Kenai National Wildlife Refuge. In winter the sport of choice here is snowmobiling, but cross-country skiers can enjoy following parts of the 80-mi. Swanson River Canoe Route or the

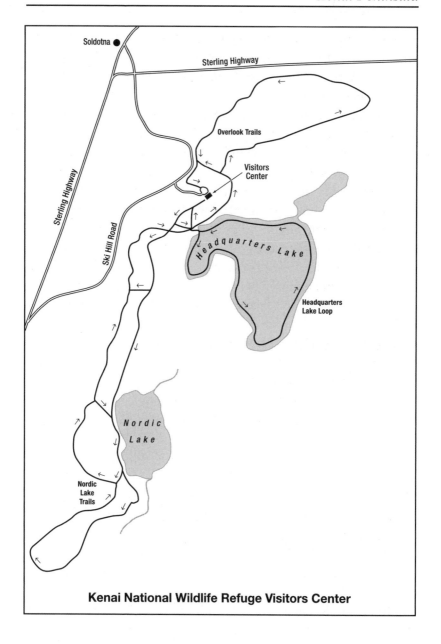

Soldotna

Sterling Highway

Overlook Trails

Visitors Center

Sterling Highway

Ski Hill Road

Headquarters Lake

Headquarters Lake Loop

Nordic Lake

Nordic Lake Trails

Kenai National Wildlife Refuge Visitors Center

60-mi. Swanson Lake Canoe Route. These are the best developed trails in the refuge and are both closed to snowmobile use. The trailheads are reachable via Swanson Lake Road and Swanson River Road, which join with the Sterling Highway just past the community of Sterling.

More easily accessible trails can be found at the Kenai National Wildlife Refuge Visitors Center. Signs on the Sterling Highway show the way to the visitors center, off Ski Hill Road less than a mile from downtown Soldotna. Trail maps, available at the center, show a 6-mi. trail system winding around two small lakes. These trails are broken out by snow machines and are suitable for touring, but are not usually groomed for either skating or diagonal skiing. The visitors center contains exhibits about the animals and plants of the refuge, and rangers there can provide information about other touring opportunities, including the Swanson River Canoe Trail system. Write to Kenai National Wildlife Refuge, P.O. Box 2139, Soldotna, AK 99669-2139 or phone 907-262-7021.

The Soldotna area in the central Kenai Peninsula has two other maintained cross-country trail systems. As a general principle, nordic skiers looking for trails outside of Anchorage or Fairbanks should seek out a local high school, because cross-country skiing is an important part of school athletic programs in Alaska.

Such is the case in Soldotna, where the best groomed trail system is adjacent to Skyview High School, two miles south of downtown Soldotna on the right side of the Sterling Highway. The Tsalteshi Ski Trails at Skyview High School consist of 2.5-km, 5-km, and 7.5-km loops groomed for both diagonal skiing and skating. These wide trails wind through tall trees, varying from gentle terrain on the inner loops to steeper hills on the outer 7.5-km loop. Skyview High School also has a small biathlon shooting range; several skiers from the Soldotna area are becoming internationally competitive biathletes. Another set of cross-country trails is at Nikiski High School, twenty-two miles north of Soldotna via the Kenai Spur Highway.

Homer Area

Homer, seventy-seven miles south of Soldotna along the Sterling Highway, is a beautiful port town looking out on Katchemak Bay. Skiing on the southern Kenai Peninsula around Homer dates back to the 1950s, when alpine ski events were included in high school competitive meets. The Katchemak Ski Club, organized to support the Homer High School ski coach and his team, installed and managed an 800-foot rope tow on the ridge above the town. Slalom events were run on the rope tow slopes, while the downhill race course descended the bluff behind Homer near the present location of East Hill Road.

In subsequent years, roads and houses have replaced the downhill course and the tow has been moved twice, finally reaching its current location near the end of Ohlson Mountain Road in the 1970s. Although the rope tow did not operate during the winters of 1995-6 and 1996-7 due to an unprecedented lack of snow, the tow has been certified for continued operation. The Katchemak Ski Club, which

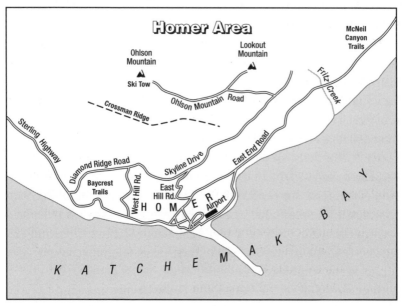

owns the eighty acres of the current downhill ski area, opens a warm-up hut and snack shop when the tow is operating. For more information, call the Katchemak Ski Club at 907-235-8304 or write to Box 1206, Homer, AK 99603.

All high school cross-country races were initially run on courses set in the rolling hills off Ohlson Mountain Road. The high school cross-country team still trains and holds some of its races in this area, where trails of any desired length and configuration can be set in the sparsely wooded country. In addition, two cross-country trail systems have been developed closer to downtown Homer.

The Baycrest Trail System is in a wooded area half a mile north of Homer, off the Sterling Highway across from the Bayview Inn. The Katchemak Nordic Ski Club (Box 44, Homer, AK 99603 or phone 907-235-6018) regularly grooms these approximately 7.5 kilometers for both striding and skating. Adjoining trails are suitable for touring into the higher country. Much of this area is within the Homer Demonstration Forest, and trail maps are posted at the forest's entrance. Attempts have been made in past years to maintain a touring trail on Crossman Ridge which would connect the Baycrest trails to the Ohlson Mountain trails, but keeping the connecting trail maintained has been difficult.

A 6-km trail system has recently been developed next to McNeil Canyon Elementary School, fifteen miles from downtown Homer on East End Road. These scenic trails overlooking Katchemak Bay are groomed for skating but do not have tracks for classical skiing. Volunteers and high school skiers are expanding the system for a total of ten kilometers of trails, arranged in 2.5-km, 7.5-km, and 10-km loops.

The rolling, sparsely wooded hills in the high country north of Homer are ideal for backcountry ski touring and telemarking, but seasoned telemarkers often seek out steeper slopes across Katchemak Bay. In the spring they take fishing boats to Halibut Cove and ski Blueberry Ridge or head to Jakolof Bay, where logging roads provide access to inviting slopes.

For more information on skiing in the Homer area, call Ohlson Mountain Sports at 907-235-5119.

ELIZABETH TOWER

Skiers using the trails at McNeil Canyon Elementary School take in spectacular views of the mountains across Katchemak Bay.

Skiing the Internet

Want to learn the latest race results, pick up tips on how to ski faster, join a ski instruction program, or enter the Tour of Anchorage? You can do all these things and more from the comfort of your home if you have access to the Internet.

Anchorage's own World Wide Web site allows you to navigate through the majority of information regarding nordic ski racing on the web. Built and maintained by skiers working with d3Systems, the site contains information in the categories of Events, Race Results, Coaching, Weather, Numbers for Ski Hotlines, Maps of the Anchorage Trail System, Links to Sites of Interest Around the Web, and Information on the Gold 2002 Ski Program.

The site was designed for Microsoft Internet Explorer, but Netscape Navigator works well too. Use your browser of choice to go to **http://www. arctic.net/xc**, or use a search engine like Yahoo to search for "Nordic Ski Racing."

Also on the local level, the Nordic Skiing Association of Anchorage's web page provides the high school competitive program with start lists and race results. High school skiers and coaches can check out the competition at **http://www. alaska.net/~nsaa/**. A similar web site from the Nordic Ski Club of Fairbanks can be reached at **http://www2. polarnet.com/~nordic**.

John Estle of the Nordic Ski Club of Fairbanks has these recommendations of non-regional sites for web skiers. His favorite place to get information about cross-country skiing or get in touch with other skiers throughout North America and the world is Usenet's **rec.skiing.nordic** newsgroup.

Cross-country Ski World, a major web page devoted to cross-country skiing, contains a broad variety of articles, tidbits, and news on all aspects of the sport. Also featured are interviews with members of the U.S. Ski Team. The site at **http://www.weblab.com/xcski/** is updated fairly regularly.

To see what it looks like to ski in the rain, visit the New England Cross-Country site at **http://www.ultranet.com/~rhaydock/**. Besides lots of race results, it displays picture albums of some of their events.

Cross-Country Canada's excellent web page has comprehensive North Ameri-can and World Cup race results and good links to information on Canadian programs for skiers and coaches. This page can be accessed at **http://canada.x-c.com/**.

At **http://www.sportsline.com/u/usskiteam/skitnews/**, the web page of the United States Ski Team deals mainly with alpine news, along with some on snowboarding, freestyle, jumping, and nordic combined.

Another of John Estle's favorite pages is maintained by Stephen Seiler, a Texan exercise physiologist living in Kristiansand, Norway. The site's numerous articles on the physiology of cross-country skiing, running, rowing, and cycling — as well as general exercise physiology — are informative without being overly technical. You can find it at **http://www.krs.hia.no/~stephens/skiing.htm**.

Each year, top skiers from around the world gather outside Valdez to compete in the World Extreme Skiing Championships.

6. Around Prince William Sound

Between the waters of Prince William Sound and the peaks of the Chugach Mountains, the port communities of Valdez and Cordova offer access to a variety of developed and undeveloped slopes. Cordova, though not connected to the state's highway systems and therefore only reachable by boat or plane, still boasts its own downhill ski area at Mt. Eyak. Three hundred miles from Anchorage via the Glenn and Richardson Highways, Valdez is becoming internationally known as the site of the World Extreme Skiing Championships, thereby attracting adventurous snowboarders and skiers.

World Extreme Skiing Championships

In 1991 several local Valdez skiers organized this competition as a way of showing off the virgin powder and steep peaks in this part of Alaska. Today the championship is a progressive three-day competition, held in late March or early April, during which thirty-five of the world's best skiers challenge the rugged slopes that surround the Tsaina Valley and Valdez.

Competitors are selected either as "wild card" entries on the basis on their extensive resumes of extreme skiing experience or through qualifying feeder events, which include the South American extremes, the European extremes, the Japanese extremes, the U.S. extremes, the all-mountain extremes, and the Alaska extremes held at Alyeska. In 1996, extreme skiers came to Valdez from Switzerland, Japan, France, Canada, Czechoslovakia, and various parts of the western United States. The 1997 competition attracted two skiers from New Zealand, and almost doubled the number of female competitors in the previous year, from six to ten.

During the three-day event, competitors choose their terrain from six different sites, each one including 45- to 60-degree slopes, on locations such as Odyssey Mountain and Wilbur Peak. A celebrity panel rates their performances according to "degree of difficulty," "style," "execution," and "grace," in addition to the novel extreme skiing qualification of "boldness and control." Snowboarders, not to be outdone, hold their own King of the Hill competition with a similar format.

Some portions of the World Extreme Skiing Championships are broadcast on television, but skiing fans wanting to get closer to the action gather along the Richardson Highway to watch with binoculars or take snow machines to the base of the mountains. One day in each competition is designated "Spectator Day" on Odyssey Mountain. More information may be obtained by writing to the office of the World Extreme Skiing Championships, P.O. Box 3309, Valdez, AK 99686 or calling 907-835-2108.

Backcountry Skiing Outside Valdez

Thanks in part to the popularity of the World Extreme Skiing Championships, the Chugach Mountains north of Valdez have gained international recognition in recent years as a place where dedicated "powder hounds" can be assured of finding rugged, untracked slopes. These mountains offer some of the world's best helicopter and snowcat skiing. Although there are no developed ski areas with tows, telemark and downhill skiers and snowboarders have found several ways to enjoy the slopes around Thompson Pass on the Richardson Highway.

Skiers and boarders are advised to start out on "The Face," also known as "The Highway Run," a stunningly beautiful 800-foot run that begins at a pullout at the crest of Thompson Pass and descends to a lower pullout at Mile 19 of the Richardson Highway. The variety of slopes along the Face make it popular with both expert and intermediate

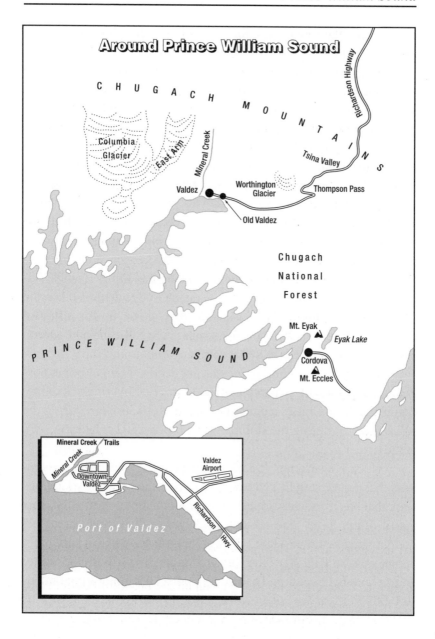

skiers. Although skiers may find it possible to hitchhike back to the top, having arrangements with a driver is recommended.

Expert skiers and boarders who are confident that they can handle steeper terrain have several options. Alaska Back Country Adventures (P.O. Box 362, Kenai, AK 99611, phone 907-835-5608 or 907-283-9354) provides guides and flies skiers in fixed-wing aircraft from the Thompson Pass airstrip on the Richardson Highway near Worthington Glacier to the top of runs with descents of 3,000 to 4,000 vertical feet. Clients will not be allowed on the plane without full avalanche equipment, including transceiver, shovels, and safety gear, all of which can be rented at the strip if necessary. Snowcats also operate from the Thompson Pass airstrip. Contact Chugach Powder Guides at P.O. Box 1865, Valdez, AK 99686; phone 907-835-2833.

Valdez Heliski Guides, owned by Doug and Emily Combs, stations a chartered ERA Helicopter at Tsaina Lodge, Mile 34.7 on the Richardson Highway. They use it to take skiers up for a day of extreme skiing, usually four to six runs. Five full-time and several part-time experienced guides accompany clients and carry full rescue equipment, including harnesses and ropes. Tsaina Lodge, now mainly a restaurant, plans to expand to provide overnight lodging. Valdez Heliski Guides can be reached at 907-835-4528 during the ski season, or during the summer at P.O. Box 25029, Jackson, WY 83001.

Valdez Heli-Camps Inc. is an all-inclusive heli-skiing operation that works with Era Helicopters to provide helicopter landings and also has a snowcat to use when the helicopters can't fly. This outfit offers three- and six-day packages with bed-and-breakfast lodging in downtown Valdez. Clients are transported to a helicopter or snowcat at Mile 20 of the Richardson Highway. With the ability to use both helicopter and snowcat, Valdez Heli-Camps guarantees 100,000 vertical feet of powder skiing in the six-day package or 50,000 feet in the three-day package. Guides and all avalanche safety equipment are provided. Additional information can be obtained by writing Valdez Heli-Camps Inc., P.O. Box 2495, Valdez, AK

99686, calling 907-783-3243, or checking the Internet at http://www.alaska.net/~heliski.

Era Helicopters (907-835-2595) also runs sight-seeing flights out of the Valdez Airport, which can be chartered by skiers or boarders who have their own guides with them. Since avalanches are a constant danger in the Chugach Mountains, where the average snowfall exceeds 400 inches, only the most knowledgeable and well-equipped skiers should venture into the area without an experienced guide.

For the most up-to-date informative on skiing conditions and services in the Valdez area, call the Valdez Convention and Visitors Bureau at 800-770-5954, or write to them at P.O. Box 1603, Valdez, AK 99686.

Mineral Creek Cross-Country Trails

The Valdez City Parks and Recreation Department maintains ten kilometers of cross-country trails that follow Mineral Creek back into the hills behind Valdez, directly behind the residential area on

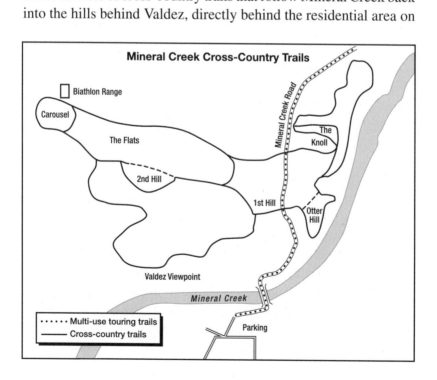

Mineral Creek Road. These trails are regularly groomed for both diagonal striding and skating. A biathlon range, not maintained by the parks department, offers four targets in winter. Call Valdez Parks and Recreation at 907-835-2531 for more information.

Dogs are not allowed on the groomed cross-country trails, but can accompany their owners on multi-use trails on the dikes along Mineral Creek. Skijoring is popular in Valdez, and a local club holds regular competitions. Call the club at 907-835-3070 for details.

Mt. Eyak Ski Area at Cordova

Southeast of Valdez along the rim of Prince William Sound, the remote community of Cordova has a surprisingly long history of downhill skiing. Around 1910, when the gold rush in Nome had diminished, some of the Scandinavian miners and businessmen there migrated to Cordova, where the Copper River and Northwestern Railway was under construction. They were joined in Cordova by relatives from the old country who brought their skis with them. The mountainous terrain and heavy snowfall of the Copper River country provided these skiers with new recreational challenges.

On January 2, 1913, the *Cordova Daily Alaskan* announced that the new Rainier Ski Club had held a 3-mi. race from downtown Cordova to an island in Eyak Lake and back; Ivar Tvjen won the race in 30 minutes and 30 seconds. Early Cordova skiers frequented the meadows on the lower slopes of Mt. Eccles that they called the "golden stairs," and fashioned ski jumps on suitable natural terrain.

The Sheriden Ski Club, formed in the 1920s, operated a rope tow at the base of Tripod Mountain above Cordova. During the winter a downtown street was closed so that the ski run could continue all the way into town. In 1972, the Sheriden Ski Club arranged to purchase one of the four original single-chair lifts from Sun Valley. These were the world's first chairlifts, built in 1936 and originally equipped with foot rests and blankets so that movie stars and other celebrities could ride up the slopes in comfort.

COURTESY OF THE CORDOVA HISTORICAL SOCIETY

Scandinavian immigrants ski the "Golden Stairs" below Mt. Eccles in 1910.

The Mt. Eyak Ski Area opened to skiers in 1976 after volunteer help provided by the Coast Guard, the Army Air National Guard, and the U.S. Forest Service installed the towers and cleared the slopes. Heavy snowfall during the first seasons made it necessary to tunnel through the snow to provide adequate clearance for the lift.

Today the Mt. Eyak Ski Area is still one of the best-kept secrets in Alaska. The base of the hill, at an elevation of 1,255 feet, is within walking distance of downtown Cordova. Its single chair, which serves five main runs with a vertical gain of 1,000 feet, is still in excellent condition with a new drive system — amenities such as blankets are no longer provided.

The terrain at Mt. Eyak is predominantly intermediate to advanced, with most skiers using trails below the midway station. The main trails are groomed with equipment recently purchased from Juneau's Eaglecrest Ski Area. Single-ride tickets can be purchased by tourists wishing to enjoy the panoramic view from the top, or by telemarkers and mountaineers planning to climb and ski the upper ridges. A rope tow services the beginners' "bunny hill" in front of the warming hut, concession stand, and rental shop.

The Mt. Eyak Ski Area is usually open weekends and Wednesdays from December to mid-April. It is still managed by the Sheriden Ski Club, which now has between 300 and 400 members. Up-to-date information is available by calling the ski club at 907-424-7766.

Cordova is not accessible by train or car, but Alaska Airlines and ERA Aviation provide regular daily flights to Cordova. Taking a stopover in Cordova on the daily jet flight between Anchorage and Juneau makes it possible to sample Mt. Eyak along with Alaska's larger downhill areas.

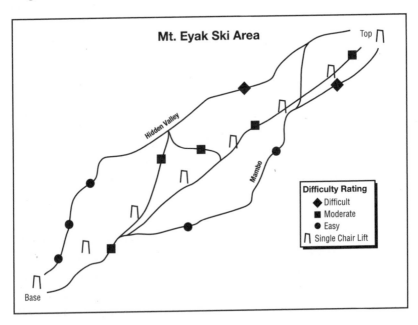

ELIZABETH TOWER

The world's oldest chairlift carries skiers to the top of Mt. Eyak Ski Area above Cordova.

Cross-Country Skiing in Cordova

Because of the area's light population and its heavy snow, cross-country skiing is not generally a priority with Cordovans. Trails do exist between Mt. Tripod and Mt. Eyak, to Crater Lake, and along Lake Eyak, but they are not regularly groomed by the Sheriden Ski Club or the U.S. Forest Service. Skiers cannot assume that these trails are being maintained. The local U.S. Forest Service Ranger Station provides information on the various trails: write to Box 280, Cordova, AK 99574 or phone 907-424-7661.

WARNING: Avalanches

Avalanches are an ever-present danger for skiers or snow-boarders in backcountry areas that do not have the extensive avalanche control programs practiced at established alpine ski areas. Backcountry guiding services provide their clients with approved avalanche rescue transceivers (beacons), and their guides carry equipment like shovels and probes for rescues. Skiers and snowboarders venturing into the mountains on their own, however, must assume responsibility for their own safety by carrying rescue equipment and learning about the factors that contribute to avalanche danger.

Avalanches occur when a snowload is so heavy it can no longer stick to a sloped mountainside. Some slope angles are more likely to produce slides than others; skiers should learn to recognize these and avoid them. The snow itself can be tested on site to see how likely it is to slide. Fresh avalanche tracks are another danger sign.

The danger of avalanches is greatest just after storms have dropped fresh loads of snow on slopes which, being near population centers, are enticing to snowboarders and telemarkers. In January 1993, two experienced "extreme skiers" decided to try new powder on the slopes of Flattop Mountain in Chugach State Park behind Anchorage. In spite of a small avalanche that knocked one of them over and tore his skis off, they continued down the slope and were caught in an avalanche that carried them 700 feet to the bottom. Although the two skiers were not buried, one of them was dashed against the rocks, severely injuring his leg.

A few weeks earlier, two men were killed while climbing on a ridge behind Flattop. Nine or ten inches of new snow had fallen a couple of days before, and seventy-mile-an-hour winds were moving the snow. Wind contributes to avalanche danger by redistributing the snow, often building it into cornices that can break and slide. Although the wind was still blowing hard, the climbers ignored all the signs of danger and began climbing in a steep gully, where an avalanche buried them in hard-packed snow.

While watching the 1995 extreme skiing championships in Thompson Pass north of Valdez, a snowboarder was killed in an avalanche. Avalanches are particularly dangerous for snowboarders, who can be pulled under by their boards because the bindings do not release.

In February 1996, during a period of heavy snowfall through-out Alaska, three experienced Fairbanks skiers died in an avalanche at Castner Glacier, about sixty miles south of Delta Junction. A snowmachiner barely cheated death that same month after an avalanche trapped him near Anton Larson Pass on Kodiak Island. The man and his companions, fortunately, were wearing transceiver beacons.

Any skier or snowboarder planning to venture into mountain-ous backcountry should learn to evaluate terrain and weather factors. One way is to attend a workshop held by the Alaska Mountain Safety Center and the Alaska Avalanche School. During the 1995-6 season, sessions were held at the University of Alaska Anchorage, Hatcher Pass in the Talkeetna Mountains, and Thompson Pass in the Chugach Mountains. The 1996-7 year also included avalanche hazard evaluation workshops in Southeastern Alaska. For more information, contact The Alaska Mountain Safety Center, 9140 Brewsters Drive, Anchorage, AK 99516. Phone/Fax: 907-345-3566.

Also, the book *Snow Sense — A Guide to Evaluating Snow Ava-lanche Hazard,* by Jill Fredston and Doug Fesler, is recommended reading.

Eaglecrest on Douglas Island, near Juneau, is a mecca for downhill skiers in Southeast Alaska.

7. SOUTHEAST ALASKA

While discussing Alaska skiing recently, a friend asked me, "Why do so many good skiers come from Juneau?" After a moment of consideration, we agreed that it's because Juneau skiers are tough. Weather patterns affecting Southeast Alaska differ significantly from those of either Southcentral or the Interior. Winter temperatures are frequently above freezing and precipitation is heavy, often in the form of rain or mixed rain and snow. Since snow cover in the coastal towns of Juneau, Sitka, and Ketchikan is not reliable, skiing must be done at higher elevations. In spite of the uncooperative weather, the City and Borough of Juneau has developed a full-service ski area of its own at Eaglecrest on Douglas Island.

Even at Eaglecrest snow conditions vary from "champagne powder" to mashed potatoes, so Juneau skiers learn to maneuver in the heavy stuff. Because of the diversity of terrain and snow conditions, locals say once you're competent on the runs at Eaglecrest, you can ski just about anywhere.

Eaglecrest is very much a local's mountain, as Juneau is not accessible by road. The occasional visiting skier from Whitehorse in the Canadian Yukon, Anchorage, Ketchikan, Sitka, or the "Lower 48" must come by plane or ferry. North of Juneau, good ski touring is found in the mountain passes outside Haines and Skagway.

The Juneau Ski Club

Founded in 1932 as an outgrowth of the Juneau Hiking Club, the Juneau Ski Club took on as one of its early tasks the placement of a 500-foot portable rope tow on Alexander Smith's mining claim in the Upper Perseverance Trail area. However, in March 1935, local skiers discovered a better area when they crossed Gastineau Channel in a dory and crashed through alders on Douglas Island until they found an open meadow.

The building of the Juneau-Douglas bridge in 1935 made development of a ski area on Douglas Island an attractive possibility. Dan Moller, a Norwegian-born skier, persuaded the Forest Service to arrange for the Civilian Conservation Corps (CCC) to build a trail to the meadow areas on Douglas Island. The Juneau Ski Club moved the little portable tow about one and a half miles up the trail, to First and Second Meadows, and the Forest Service erected shelters, which became known as First Cabin and Second Cabin. However, skiers still had to shoulder their skis and hike three miles up the Dan Moller Trail to reach this primitive ski area.

In the early 1950s, the ski club moved the tow to a higher site, known as the Douglas Ski Bowl, and built a warming hut. It also acquired a Trucker SnowCat, christened "Oola," that could carry forty to fifty skiers with a sled caboose. Snowcats provided three trips per day to the upper tow and to a commercially operated tow on Second Meadow until Eaglecrest opened in 1976.

Today the Juneau Ski Club runs a Junior Alpine Racing program and publishes a skiing newsletter. It can be reached by writing to Box 32358, Juneau, AK 99803.

Eaglecrest Ski Area

In the late 1960s the Juneau Ski Club, faced with the decision of whether to expand the Douglas Ski Bowl and build a road to it, started looking at other options. Bob Janes and Craig Lindh, both

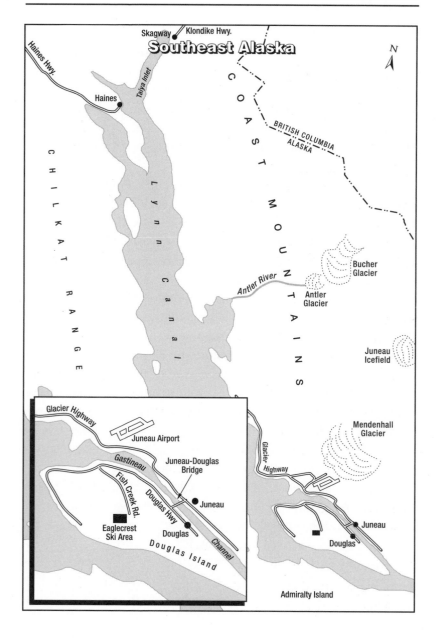

employees of the U.S. Forest Service and expert skiers, scouted Douglas Island and recommended that instead a new ski area be built at a site called the Fish Creek Drainage. In 1971, Alaska's congressional delegation secured a $950,000 appropriation, which was matched by the Bureau of Outdoor Recreation, for construction of an access road. Juneau Ski Club members were able to sell local voters on approving a one percent increase in their sales tax to build the Eaglecrest Ski Area.

Lift construction began in 1975. The following year, the ski area opened with a day lodge, a platter lift, and the Hooter chairlift, which serves the novice slopes and the Hilda cross-country trail. The Ptarmigan lift, which takes skiers to 3,000-foot Pittman Ridge and gives access to two open bowls and miles of steep glade and tree skiing, was added two years later.

All of Eaglecrest's 630 acres are owned and operated by the city and borough of Juneau. Municipal employees run the ski school, food service, rental shop, ski patrol, and weekend bus service. Eaglecrest usually has to be subsidized by the city because the proceeds from its approximately 50,000 skier visits per year do not cover its operating costs. Most residents, however, consider it a good investment because of the winter recreation it offers the people of Juneau.

A vast arena of out-of-bounds skiing exists just beyond the ski area boundary for skiers and snowboarders who want bigger, steeper, more dangerous terrain. Eaglecrest has an open out-of-bounds policy, but numerous signs point out that people venturing into the hinterlands do so at their own risk. Eaglecrest neither patrols nor conducts avalanche control beyond its boundary.

Eaglecrest's rental shop carries a full line of equipment, including both alpine and nordic skis and snowboards. Snowboards are very popular with all ages at Eaglecrest because they are often easier than skis to control in the wet, heavy, loose snow.

A daily $7 trail fee allows nordic skiers access to two cross-

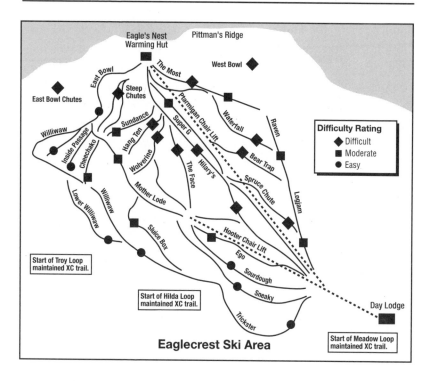

Eaglecrest Ski Area

country trails, groomed for both diagonal and skating techniques, and two rides up the Hooter Chair to reach the Hilda Trail. Eaglecrest has the only regularly groomed cross-country trails in the Juneau area because the snow cover in town is not reliable. However, the nonprofit Nordic Ski Club occasionally sets cross-country trails in the Mendenhall Valley when the snow is good.

Eaglecrest is open five days a week, Thursday through Monday, from roughly November to April depending on the snowfall. For more information, call the Eaglecrest Business Office at 907-586-5284, or for snow conditions call 907-586-5330.

The Ski to Sea Relay, held in April each year, is a popular Eaglecrest event, drawing as many as 100 to 130 teams. Each team consists of a downhill skier, a cross-country skier, two runners, and a biker. The downhill skier starts at the top of Eaglecrest and skis down to the cross-country trail at the base of the mountain. Those three kilometers of trail are covered by a nordic skier, who hands off to the winter runner. That first runner races halfway down Eaglecrest Road (about three kilometers), then passes the baton to the spring runner, who covers three kilometers to reach the North Douglas Highway. The bicycler then rides the last six miles of the race to False Outer Point. For more details on this unusual race, call Foggy Mountain Sports Store, 907-586-6780.

We've Come a Long Way!

Alaskan women have made great contributions to competitive skiing over the past twenty-five years, as revealed by the story of a few top female skiers.

Barbara Boochever was a senior at Juneau Douglas High School in 1963 when she won the Alaska State Women's Cross-Country Ski Championship at the Anchorage Fur Rendezvous. Boochever and another Juneau girl, along with two boys, were named to represent Alaska in the Junior National Cross-Country Ski Championships at Jackson Hole, Wyoming, even though there was no sanctioned race for girls there.

The previous year two Juneau girls, Ann Pym and Joan Gissberg, had competed with the boys in the cross-country races at Steamboat Springs, in an effort to open the door for U.S. women in future Olympic and International cross-country ski events. Pym and Gissberg had matched up well with their male counterparts in Alaska, but they were not competitive with boys at the national races in 1962. Therefore girls were not welcomed at the Junior National races in 1963, and Barbara Boochever did not have the opportunity to compete.

In those days, girls in Juneau competed in alpine as well as nordic events, and Boochever

"Out of Bounds" Helicopter Skiing

The snowcapped Coast and Chilkat Mountains around Juneau have proven a temptation to intrepid skiers and snowboarders. Out of Bounds Adventures, a Juneau-based helicopter tour company, has received U.S. Forest Service permission to take helicopter ski tours to three areas around Juneau and make helicopter landings on five glaciers around Haines. The tour company takes skiers to slopes in the Chilkat Mountains, near Antler River, on Antler Glacier, on Bucher Glacier, and at the Juneau Icefield. For more information, contact Bruce Griggs at 907-789-7008.

went on to race for Cornell while attending college.

Cross-country ski boosters in Alaska did not give up easily. They continued to press for national sanctioning of events for women. In 1966, Colonel Eric Wikner, a founder of the Nordic Ski Club of Anchorage, wrote to other United States Ski Association divisions, urging them to join Alaska in promoting women's cross-country races. Thanks to a strong school-based ski program, Alaska was a step ahead of the rest of the United States in 1967 when girls' cross-country races were finally sanctioned by the USSA. Three girls from Anchorage, Barbara Britch, Sharon Strutz, and Jane Whitmore, swept both individual and relay races at Junior Nationals in Duluth, Minnesota.

Barbara Britch continued to dominate women's cross-country racing on the national level for several years, being named to the first U.S. women's team in 1969. She and Margie Mahoney from Anchorage competed in the 1972 Olympics in Sapporo, Japan, and Alaskan women have competed in all of the subsequent Winter Olympics. Scandinavian and Russian women still dominate in international races, but Nina Kempel from Anchorage, who competed in the 1994 Winter Games, is training in Scandinavia for the 1998 Olympics. She's doing

Backcountry Skiing Around Haines and Skagway

Juneau residents call the area at the head of Lynn Canal their "sun belt." Since the mountain passes north of Haines and Skagway tend to have consistent snow cover and better winter weather than Juneau, locals often head up to Haines by plane or ferry for ski touring and snowboarding.

Alaska Backcountry Outfitters in Haines specializes in providing ski, snowshoe, and snowboard rentals, and guiding tours into the mountains around Chilkat Pass on the Haines Highway. Miles and miles of good touring and telemark terrain are accessible from the highway, and the Haines store (formerly called Telemark Line Ski Outfitters) can arrange transportation to the 3,304-foot pass and pick-up at a lower elevation.

something that American women aren't expected to do there — she's winning races!

Alaskan women broke into international competition in alpine events in 1988 when Hilary Lindh, daughter of Barbara Boochever and Craig Lindh, competed in the Calgary Olympics. She had started skiing in Juneau before she was six, even though she had to hike about a thousand feet up to the rope tow at Third Cabin. When Eaglecrest Ski Area opened in 1976, Lindh had a challenging mountain on which to improve her skills. By the age of thirteen she could beat all the local competition.

After two years of training at Rowmark Academy in Salt Lake City, Lindh captured the World Junior Downhill Championship at age sixteen. In addition to winning several World Cup downhill races, Hilary received international acclaim by winning a silver medal in the downhill race at the Albertville Winter Olympics in 1992. Both Hilary and Megan Gerety of Anchorage raced in the 1994 Olympics and the 1996 World Cup circuit.

Lindh was sidelined with an ankle injury and unable to

Also, tracks are sometimes set on thirty kilometers of cross-country trail in the Alaska Chilkat Bald Eagle Preserve by members of the Haines Ski Club. For additional information, call the ski club at 907-766-2876. Anyone planning to ski in this area is reminded to bring identification with them, preferably a passport, since many favorite skiing locations including Chilkat Pass are in Canada.

The Haines Highway and the Klondike Highway between Whitehorse and Skagway are both maintained throughout the winter. Skiers from Whitehorse often use the area in White Pass along the Klondike Highway north of Skagway for cross-country racing. The Buckwheat Classic, held in mid-March, features 10-km, 25-km, and 50-km races that attract some of Canada's leading nordic skiers.

compete in the U.S. Alpine Championships in 1996, but Gerety and nineteen-year-old Kjersti Bjorn-Roli from Anchorage placed second and third respectively in both downhill and super-G slalom races. Both these young skiers are products of the Mt. Alyeska Mighty Mites and the Junior Racing Program sponsored by Alyeska Ski Club. The national female snowboarding champion, Rosie Fletcher from Girdwood, also claims Alyeska as her home mountain.

Hilary Lindh returned to the international racing scene in 1997, capturing the World Downhill Championship and then both the U.S. National Downhill and Super-G Championships.

At the age of twenty-seven, after thirteen years on the U.S. Ski Team, Lindh has retired at the top of her career and is now a full-time student at the University of Utah.

Since Megan Gerety joined Lindh on the podium as silver medal winner in both the National Downhill and Super-G races, Alaska still has a top woman alpine competitor ready for the 1998 Olympics in Japan.

Cross-country trails wind around Winter Lake Lodge, located along the historic Iditarod Trail.

8. THE BACKCOUNTRY EXPERIENCE

For the adventurous skier, Alaska presents several ways to enjoy the backcountry. Alpine and telemark skiers can take advantage of helicopter, fixed wing, or snowcat guide services operating at Hatcher Pass, Alyeska, Valdez, and Juneau. Nordic ski clubs in Anchorage and Fairbanks organize weekend touring programs throughout the area. And both ski lodges and public service cabins are available for rent along wilderness trail systems.

Backcountry Ski Lodges

Several remote lodges in various parts of Alaska attract skiers in the winter by preparing trails for touring. Following is a list of some of these favorite skiing getaways that maintain their own cross-country trails. In addition, many bed-and-breakfasts and other hostelries in Alaskan cities and small towns provide access to the downhill ski areas and public cross-country trail systems. Tourism is at a low ebb in Alaska during the winter, and skiers often are welcomed with lower rates and attractive package programs.

The Anchorage Convention and Visitors Bureau has compiled a Winter Products Catalogue and can provide more information on winter vacation opportunities for skiers throughout Alaska. Contact the visitors bureau at 524 W. 4th Ave., Anchorage, AK 99501-2212. Phone 907-276-4118 or fax 907-278-5559. You can also visit their Internet website at http://www.alaska.net/~acvb or send e-mail to acvb@alaska.net.

Denali View Chalet: For many years Sepp and Brigitte Weber have pleased Southcentral cross-country skiers with the Austrian hospitality and cuisine at their wilderness lodge with a spectacular view of Mt. McKinley and the Alaska Range. Sepp carries gear by snow machine while guests ski eight miles to the lodge from a parking lot on Petersville Road, which turns off the Parks Highway about 120 miles north of Anchorage at Trappers Creek. The lodge, which can accommodate twenty people, is surrounded by forty kilometers of groomed trails for skiers of all abilities. For more information, call 907-345-2081 or write to Sepp and Brigitte Weber, P.O. Box 111663, Anchorage, AK 99511-1663.

Winter Lake Lodge: The proprietors of Riversong Lodge, noted for its summer fishing and gourmet cooking, Carl and Kirsten Dixon have recently opened a winter lodge at the Finger Lake checkpoint on the Iditarod Trail. Kirsten loves to cook and Carl likes to ski, so they are a natural team for hosting a fly-in ski weekend. Besides skiing along the historic Iditarod Trail, guests have access to about sixteen kilometers of challenging cross-country ski trails set by Carl. For more information, contact Riversong Adventures, 2463 Cottonwood St., Anchorage, AK 99508 or phone 907-274-2710. Fax 907-277-6256.

Majestic Valley Lodge: The Talcott family operates Majestic Valley Lodge at Mile 115 on the Glenn Highway, north of Anchorage in the pass between the Chugach and Talkeetna Mountains. The lodge and bunkhouse, which can accommodate twenty people, is located just below treeline at 3,000 feet — in light, dry snow — near Gunsight Mountain. Amenities include creative, homemade meals and use of a wood-stove sauna.

The Talcotts groom up to thirty kilometers of trails seven feet wide, portions of which parallel the canyon leading to Matanuska Glacier. Majestic Valley Lodge can also provide skiers with access to the trails formerly maintained by Sheep Mountain Lodge and to telemark slopes on Gunsight Mountain. A twenty-passenger

COURTESY OF WINTER LAKE LODGE

A young skier tries out her equipment outside Winter Lake Lodge.

motorcoach is available to transport guests to and from the lodge upon request. Information about rates and snow conditions can be obtained by writing to Majestic Valley Lodge, HC03 8514(b), Palmer, AK 99645. Phone 907-746-2930 or fax 907-746-2931.

The Resort at Chena Hot Springs, on Chena Hot Springs Road thirty miles northeast of Fairbanks, can accommodate up to 150 people and is open throughout the winter. An oasis for Interior Alaskans since 1905, Chena Hot Springs features a solarium with large spring-fed pools, hot tubs, and spas, in addition to twenty miles of ski trails for all skill levels. Round trip transportation from Fairbanks can be arranged. For reservations or more information, contact the marketing director at P.O. Box 73440, Fairbanks, AK 99707-3440. Phone 907-452-7867 or fax 907-456-3122.

Renting Public-Use Cabins

Skiers looking for an affordable way to get away to the wilderness should also consider the cabins maintained by state and federal agencies in Alaska. These public recreation cabins offer rugged accommodations, usually a heating stove, bunks or sleeping platforms, table and chairs, and an outhouse. Renters are responsible for providing their own food, cook stove, cooking utensils, water, and bedding. Skiers traveling in Alaska's backcountry must take responsibility for their own safety and should be prepared with survival skills and proper equipment.

Generally, cabin permits are issued on a first-come/first-served basis for noncommercial purposes to anyone over eighteen years old. However, because of high demand, some agencies use a lottery system to determine who gets to use them. Several different public agencies, each with its own guidelines for rental, manage cabins with winter trail access.

The U.S. Forest Service manages nine cabins along the Resurrection Pass Trail between Hope and Copper Landing on the Kenai Peninsula, and four cabins on the Russian Lakes and Resurrection

River trails. Forest Service cabins on Prince William Sound are not accessible by trail, but transportation via sailboat may soon be available through Sound Eco Adventures (P.O. Box 242291, Anchorage, AK 99524). In 1997, user fees were $25 per night, with a maximum stay of seven nights during the winter. For reservations, write to Alaska Public Lands Information Center, 605 W. 4th Ave., Suite 105, Anchorage, AK 99501. Phone 907-271-2599.

The National Park Service maintains one cabin at Exit Glacier, off the Seward Highway north of Seward. Open for public use only in the winter, when the Exit Glacier Road is closed, the Exit Glacier cabin may be reached by ski, dogsled, and snow machine. Cabin fees in 1997 were $30 per night with a three-night limit. For reservations, write to Alaska Public Lands Information Center, 605 W. 4th Ave., Suite 105, Anchorage, AK 99501. Phone 907-271-2737.

Alaska State Parks manages five cabins in the Chena River State Recreation Area, located between Miles 26 and 51 on Chena Hot Springs Road northeast of Fairbanks. The cabins provide access to the Chena Hot Springs winter multi-use trail and to 2-km and 5-km maintained cross-country ski trails at Twin Bears Camp.

Along the Parks Highway eighty miles north of Anchorage, the Nancy Lake State Recreation Area, which also has a series of winter trails, contains twelve state park cabins that each sleep from four to eight people. Two other Alaska State Parks cabins are at Byers Lake in Denali State Park, near Trapper Creek on the Parks Highway.

Rates in 1997 ranged from $25 to $35 per night, with maximum stays of three to five nights. The cabins can be rented from the nearest state park office or from the Department of Natural Resources Public Information Center, 3601 C Street, Suite 200, Anchorage, AK 99503-5929. Phone 907-269-8400.

The Bureau of Land Management (BLM) owns ten cozy log cabins built at scenic locations along over 200 miles of winter trail in the White Mountains National Recreation Area north of Fairbanks. The cabins must be reserved and can be booked up to thirty days in advance. Fees in 1997 were $20 per night on weekends and $15 during the week, with a three-night limit. For reservations, write to the Bureau of Land Management, Land Information Office, 1150 University Avenue, Fairbanks, AK 99709-3844. Phone 907-474-2251.

Heli-skiing and Snowcat Services

As backcountry skiing and snowboarding have become increasingly popular in Alaska, helicopter and snowcat operators have expanded their facilities to accommodate the demand, which has been spurred by the extreme skiing and snowboarding championships held yearly in the Chugach Mountains north of Valdez. Available backcountry heli-skiing and snowcat operations, described elsewhere in this book, are summarized here.

Anchorage (Girdwood - Alyeska)

Chugach Powder Guides, operating from the Girdwood airstrip with ERA Helicopters, has a Forest Service permit to access virgin powder on 450 square miles of Chugach Mountain slopes on the Kenai Peninsula southeast of Girdwood. Skiers, who are guaranteed 16,000-20,000 vertical feet of skiing a day, are provided with avalanche beacons and accompanied by experienced guides. Chugach Powder Guides, which is also seeking a permit to transport skiers up the Girdwood valley by snowcat, works closely with Alyeska Resort. Phone 907-783-4354.

Hatcher Pass

Glacier SnowCat Skiing Tours, Inc. (P.O. Box 874234, Wasilla, AK 99687) advertises safe, affordable backcountry skiing and snowboarding with access to as much as 20,000 vertical feet of untracked powder daily. These slopes are in the Talkeetna Mountains, where snow is usually lighter and dryer than snow in the coastal Chugach Range. The snowcat, which can accommodate twelve passengers, a ski patroller, and the driver, boards at the Motherlode Lodge at the base of Hatcher Pass. All clients are provided with avalanche beacons and instruction in backcountry safety procedures.

Valdez (Richardson Highway - Thompson Pass)

Headquartered at Tsaina Lodge, Mile 34.7 of the Richardson Highway north of Valdez, Valdez Heliski Guides uses a chartered ERA helicopter to transport skiers to slopes around Thompson Pass. Owned by Doug and Emily Combs, the company employs full-time and part-time experienced guides to accompany their clients with full rescue equipment. Tsaina Lodge also has a restaurant and is expanding to provide overnight lodging. Phone 907-835-4528.

Fixed-wing aircraft and snowcats also operate out of the Thompson Pass airstrip on the Richardson Highway near Worthington Glacier. Alaska Back Country Adventures transports clients using fixed-wing aircraft from the Thompson Pass airstrip (P.O. Box 362, Kenai, AK 99611, phone 907-835-5608 or 907-283-9354). Valdez Heliski Guides provides helicopter service mainly for the World Extreme Skiing Championships. Valdez Heli-Camps provides helicopter and/or snowcat skiing and houses clients at bed-and-breakfasts in Valdez (P.O. Box 2495, Valdez, AK 99686, phone 907-783-3243). Valdez Recreation Co-op, combining Chugach Power Cats and Glacier SnoCats, depends on snowcats to transport skiers (907-783-4354).

Juneau

Out of Bounds Adventures, with top-of-the-line A-star helicopters, offers skiers and snowboarders access to 3,000-4,000 foot runs in the Chilkat Mountains and 2,000-4,000 vertical foot runs in the 1,500-square-mile Juneau Icefield, which receives 100 feet of annual snowfall. Out of Bounds works under permit from the U.S. Forest Service and can be reached at P.O. Box 020862, Juneau, AK 99802. Phone 907-789-7008 or 1-800-HELLYEA. Fax 907-789-7287.

NORWAY 1970

Our family gained a new perspective on nordic skiing in the winter of 1970 when my husband and I, along with our twelve-year-old son and nine-year-old daughter, joined a Nordic Ski Club trip to Norway.

On a Saturday morning we boarded the train in Bergen and were amazed at the huge crowd of Norwegians preparing for a ski weekend, many of them carrying camping gear.

Our first stop was Finse, reported to be a training ground for polar expeditions. We endured severe weather, but skiers at the hostel run by the Norwegian Ski Touring organization accepted us warmly — partly because they were convinced that Alaska was part of Canada rather than the United States.

Back in Alaska, such tree-less slopes would have been a playground for snow machines, but in Norway snow machines were used only for trail maintenance and mountain rescue. Wands at intervals along the established trails allowed skiers to find their way even in thick, blowing snow.

One day we took the train to an alpine ski area at Voss and were gratified that we could ski the easier trails with our touring skis.

Ski lifts at Voss and Geilo provided access to maintained touring trails between villages, so we could ski from village to village and return to our home base by bus. Farmhouses along the way provided shelter and hot cranberry drinks.

Our final stop was Nordmark, a large ski park on the outskirts of Oslo. We skied in to a hostel inside the park while snow machines transported our gear. During our week in Nordmark, we watched the Holmenkollen ski jumping and cross-country races; participants included an Alaskan girl, Barbara Britch, and several Native skiers from Inuvik, Canada. We were amazed by the crowds of fans along the trails, cheering for the skiers. Packed city buses equipped with ski racks transported the Oslo residents to the trails.

In Norway, nordic ski champions, rather than football or basketball players, were featured in advertisements. Store windows exhibited equipment for ski tours, which would be the most popular activity during the upcoming Easter holidays.

Coming home with a new appreciation for skiing as a northern way of life, we realized what tremendous potential skiing might have in Alaska. (Another benefit of the trip was losing ten pounds, because of the unaccustomed daily exercise and Spartan diet.)

Over the ensuing twenty-five years, much of this potential has been realized in Alaska — but not quite in a Scandinavian manner. The countryside in Alaska is more rugged and less developed than that in Scandinavia. Ski parks in Anchorage and Fairbanks rival Nordmark and have hosted international races, but our city buses aren't equipped with ski racks. Alaskans can't ski from farmhouse to farmhouse, but Forest Service cabins are for rent along winter trails. Several backcountry lodges maintain ski trails and provide meals that are more appetizing to Alaskans than goat cheese and lefse.

Glossary of Skiing Place Names

Anchorage Nordic

Hillside Park

Besh Lighted Loop — Named for Tom Besh, an early Anchorage junior high and high school cross-country competitor who was a University of Alaska Anchorage cross-country ski coach until his untimely death in an airplane accident.

Richter Loop — Named for Don and Marion Richter, parents of Service High School cross-country skiers Ronnie and Pam. They were some of the Nordic Ski Club members who helped build the first Hillside Park ski trails.

Spencer Loop — Named for Bill Spencer, a former Olympic cross-country competitor who designed this 7.5-km trail. He has succeeded Tom Besh as the University of Alaska Anchorage's cross-country ski coach.

Kincaid Park

Kim Berg Biathlon Range — Named for the contractor who contributed the material and the labor to build the range.

Lekisch Trail System — These challenging, competitive trails were designed and built in memory of Andrew Lekisch, a promising young athlete who died as a result of a fall while on a training run in the Chugach Mountains in 1987.

Margaux's Loop — This 5-km lighted loop has been named in memory of Margaux Meneker, a promising high school cross-country skier who died in a tragic home accident in 1996.

Mize Loop — Named for Dick Mize, a former Olympic cross-country and biathlon competitor, who was a cross-country ski coach and principal at Dimond High School. He was instrumental in designing and building most of the Kincaid Park ski trails and is still an active competitor in Master's races.

Sisson Trail — Was developed by friends as a memorial to Alex Sisson, who participated in all types of skiing in the Anchorage area.

Alyeska Resort

Von Imhoff Drive — Named for Chris Von Imhoff, manager of Alyeska Resort.

Jim's Branch — This new expert trail on the north face of Alyeska Mountain has been named for Jim Branch, Alyeska's first manager.

Max's Mountain — Although this flat peak adjacent to Alyeska Mountain was officially named for Ernie Bauman, who used to land skiers on the mountain in his light plane, it is commonly referred to as Max's Mountain. The Alyeska public information staff indicates that Max was a skier who was taken to the top of the mountain by helicopter and then beat the helicopter down.

Tanaka Lift — This chairlift was installed in 1979 to serve the racing program and was named in memory of Jim Tanaka, who helped organize and run the Alyeska Mighty Mite racing program before his untimely death from a heart attack.

Fairbanks Nordic

Skarland Trail System — Named for Dr. Ivar Skarland, the University of Alaska Fairbanks anthropology professor who was a pioneer in the development of cross-country ski trails at the university.

Jim Whisenhant Ski Trails — On March 15, 1997, the Birch Hill Recreation Area ski trails were officially dedicated in honor of Jim Whisenhant, former cross-country ski coach at Lathrop High School, who was instrumental in designing and building the trails.

Eaglecrest Ski Area

Janes Niehues — Named for Bob Janes, long-time Juneau skier and historian for the Juneau Ski Club.

Hilary's — Named in honor of Olympic skier Hilary Lindh.

Index

Index

P

Palmer 69, 70, 74
Prince William Sound 13, 123, 149
public-use cabins 95, 113, 148–150

R

Recreational Equipment Inc. (REI) 33
Resort at Chena Hot Springs, The 148
Resurrection Pass Trail 113, 148
Russian Jack Springs Park 17, 28, 32, 37
Ruth Glacier 79, 80, 81

S

Salcha Trails 92
Seppala, Leonhard 10
Seward Highway 113–114
Sheriden Ski Club 128
Sitka 135
Skagway 142
Skarland, Ivar 86–88, 89
Skarland Ski Trail System 88–90
ski jumping 37–38
Ski to Sea Relay 139
skijoring 38–40
Skiland 85, 100–102
snowboarding 13, 36, 52, 55, 74, 123, 124, 133, 138
Snowcat services 150–151
Soldotna 114, 116
Sound Eco Adventures 149
Southeast Alaska 135-143
sporting goods stores
  Beaver Sports 90, 91
  Gary King Sporting Goods 24–25
Sterling Highway 114–116
Swanson Lake Canoe Route 116
Swanson River Canoe Route 114

T

Talkeetna 81, 82, 108
Talkeetna Mountains 17, 69, 150
Thompson Pass 124
Tincan Mountain 107
Tony Knowles Coastal Trail 17, 30
Tour of Anchorage 20–21, 23, 31
Tripod Mountain 128
Turnagain Pass 113
Two Rivers Trails 90

U

UAA Alaska Wilderness Studies Program 34
University of Alaska Fairbanks 86–90
University Park Trails 90

V

Valdez 123-128, 145, 151
Valdez Heli-Camps 126, 151
Valdez Heliski Guides 126, 151

W

White Mountains National Recreation Area 95, 150
Winter Lake Lodge 146
World Extreme Skiing Championships 123–124, 133

TOWER FAMILY

About the Author

When Drs. John and Elizabeth Tower left New Haven, Connecticut, in 1954 to establish the first private pediatric practice in the Territory of Alaska, they brought wooden Northland skis with them and joined the Anchorage Ski Club to use the Arctic Valley rope tows. By contributing money for building the first T-bar tow, they became life members of the Anchorage Ski Club. They skied Mt. Alyeska by helicoptor before the resort there was developed.

During ski weekends in bunkhouses at Independence Mine, the Tower family watched U.S. Army biathlon skiers training, and acquired their first cross-country skis. While Elizabeth was pursuing a twenty-five year career as a physician with the Alaska State Division of Public Health, she became a charter member of the Nordic Ski Club of Anchorage and served as its president in 1970. Since retirement from the medical profession in 1986, she has developed an interest in Alaska history and published several books. Three Tower children and six grandchildren live in Anchorage and are active in the Nordic Skiing Association of Anchorage, the Junior Nordic League, the Alyeska Ski Club, and the Alyeska Mighty Mite program.